Life Alone Devo

365 Hope-Filled Devotions
To Help You Consistently
Draw Closer To Jesus And
Grow In Your Faith Daily

Jimmy Akers

Hey, friend! Please read this first.

Dear YOU,

I wrote this devotional book for YOU! But it turns out, I also wrote this devotional book for me.

For almost 7 years I wrote and worked on this labor of love. 365 different devotional thoughts with scripture, prayer and application, plus 1 for leap year is a lot y'all! But with a ton of prayer, intentionality and hard work over the years, I believe it is going to be a blessing. At least I hope so!

Years ago I was the lead pastor of a new church plant in York, PA. It ended up being one of the most amazing experiences of my life which ended up also leading to one of the most painful seasons of my life. That's another book entirely, but context is important.

Starting a new church is hard! Like, don't do it unless Jesus makes it abundantly clear that you can't do anything else, kind of hard. But you also get to see God do amazing things in the process! One of those things was connecting with people that were completely new to church, faith, Jesus, all of it!

I grew up in church, but in most cases it seemed like we did church really well for church people. But I wanted people to know about the hope that Jesus brought into my life, especially people that had never experienced God in that kind of way. Of course I wanted to help followers of Jesus grow in their faith, but also focus attention on people that were on a new faith journey and help them grow in their faith and relationship with Jesus.

In order for most plants, fruit, and vegetables to grow, they need certain elements. Important things like, seeds, soil, water and sunshine. I know there are others and some don't need all of these things, but most do. Faith and a relationship with Jesus also need some important elements in order to grow.

Along with relationships and community, worship, prayer and time in the Bible are important elements in our faith journey.

But I found out that many of our friends that were new to faith, struggled with reading the bible and praying on a regular basis. It turns out, that's pretty true for people that have claimed to follow Jesus for a long time as well.

Many devotionals (books focused on spiritual growth), that I came across at that time were overly complicated and hard to process, or just not enough. Like many other popular books that are published, many devotionals are not even written by the big names on the cover.

I struggled with reading and comprehension myself growing up, so I decided to try and write a devotional that I probably would have read when I got serious about my faith as a teenager. Recently I heard author and speaker Rory Vaden on a podcast interview with Jon Acuff say, "You are most powerfully positioned to serve the person you once were." So here we are!

Earlier I wrote that this devotional book is for you, but I ended up writing it for me too. If you spend intentional time writing, praying, researching and thinking about scripture for a long time, you also grow in your faith and relationship with Jesus.

So I do hope this book blesses you, and of course I want it to put a smile on the face of Jesus. But it's also a snapshot from 7 years of my life, while I was trying to hold on to Jesus and help others know him more even while I was also walking through an incredible amount of pain and change in my life.

Psalm 46:1 reminds us that God is an ever-present help in times of trouble. And He is! He still is!! And that's the God I want you to know and fall in love with. And one way to do that is with time in scripture, prayer, and with applying those things.

In John 15:5 Jesus reminds us how important it is to stay connected to Him when He says, "I am the vine; you are the branches. If you remain in me and I in you, you will bear much fruit; apart from me you can do nothing."

So if we will respond to His invitation to connect with Him and stay connected to Him, we will bear much fruit. In other words, our life will be better if we remain connected to God. This was once going to be called the Remain Devo for that very reason.

I wrote this devotional to create space for us to intentionally connect with Jesus through scripture, a brief thought, prayer and application. What you have in your hands is 365 hope-filled devotions to help you consistently draw closer to Jesus and grow in your faith daily. I pray it is an encouragement to you.

This devotional book is laid out intentionally. It starts with 1 verse. If you don't typically read the bible but read that 1 verse a day, you've got 365 verses in for the year. Better than none!

At the bottom of each page there are 4 scripture references in a one year read through the bible format. The verse of the day came out of that reading. But if you want to go further, read those references and you will read through the entire bible in a year. The entire daily devo will take about 15 minutes a day to read if you read those references and if you read as slow as me.

Then there is the devotional thought that I wrote to correspond with the verse of the day, and a brief prayer and 2 application questions. It would not be a bad idea to keep a journal to respond to the 2 questions. But that's all up to you!

The hashtags #DontDoLifeAloneDevo and #ReadPrayApplyRemain are also included on every page. They are a reminder of what you are doing, but also there to remind you to share this with others. If a particular day sticks out to you, post it on social media with those hashtags. And years from now if hashtags fall off the cliff and mean nothing again, don't discount them! They may make a comeback like mullets and fanny packs are right now! If you don't know what I'm talking about, let's move on.

This, Don't Do Life Alone Devo, is for YOU!

Now, read, pray, apply and remain!

This is what you are about to do. And I promise, if you spend time reading the Bible and processing it with the devotional thought, praying about it and then figuring out how to apply it in your life, you will grow in your faith and your relationship with Jesus. Because this is not my idea, it's His!

God never intended for us to do life alone. So do this with a friend, or your spouse, child or even your entire family. Get some people together and form a small group. Meet up weekly to discuss what you took away from the weeks readings, or connect with friends online where you can exchange messages to encourage each other.

If this is helpful at all, please go on Amazon and write a review and tell people about it. I'm not just telling you this because I want to sell more books. I mean I do! But the impact is more important than the dollars. This book is 7 years worth of writing, praying and processing that developed over my 39 years so far on this planet and my own personal faith journey. There is a lot invested in this. And my prayer is, that you receive the blessings from all of that.

So I wrote this devotional book for me, but I also wrote it for YOU. For us!

Let's take some intentional next steps together. Let's work through the pages of this book, processing God's word, spending some time in prayer and working to apply it as God leads us.

It does not matter what day you start reading it, just start! God is ready to meet you where you are, when you're ready. You are loved! Your best days are ahead, friend. God is not finished with your story.

Don't do life alone.

-jimmy

January 1

'"Behold, the virgin shall be with child, and bear a Son, and they shall call His name Immanuel,' which is translated, 'God with us.'" Matthew 1:23

Jesus is Immanuel, God with us. What would happen if we lived like this was true? Make an intentional decision today and everyday to acknowledge Jesus and make room for Him to work in your life.

Thank you God for another day and for your word. Help me process it, live it and share it. In Jesus' name I pray, amen.

What is God speaking to you? What action will you take in light of today's devotion?

#DontDoLifeAloneDevo #ReadPrayApplyRemain

Genesis 1-2, Psalms 1:1-6, Proverbs 1:1-6, Matthew 1-2:12

January 2

"If you do well, will you not be accepted? And if you do not do well, sin lies at the door. And its desire is for you, but you should rule over it." Genesis 4:7

Today will bring plenty of opportunities your way. You can't always control your circumstances, but you can control how you respond. Don't allow sin to dictate how you live. Pray first, let God lead you and walk through the day victoriously.

Thank you God for another day and for your word. Help me process it, live it and share it. In Jesus' name I pray, amen.

What is God speaking to you? What action will you take in light of today's devotion?

#DontDoLifeAloneDevo #ReadPrayApplyRemain

Genesis 3-4, Psalms 2:1-12, Proverbs 1:7-9, Matthew 2:13-3:6

January 3

"I lay down and slept; I awoke, for the LORD sustained me." Psalms 3:5

Who woke you up this morning? How did you make it through that situation that you thought for sure was going to crush you? The truth is, God sustains us. He sustains us so much; it can be hard to keep up.

Thank you God for another day and for your word. Help me process it, live it and share it. In Jesus' name I pray, amen.

What is God speaking to you? What action will you take in light of today's devotion?

#DontDoLifeAloneDevo #ReadPrayApplyRemain

Genesis 5-7, Psalms 3:1-8, Proverbs 1:10-19, Matthew 3:7-4:11

January 4

"Wisdom calls aloud outside; She raises her voice in the open squares." Proverbs 1:20

We live in a day and age where there is no shortage of information, but what are we doing with it? James 1:5 reminds us that God gives wisdom generously to all who ask. Never stop growing.

Thank you God for another day and for your word. Help me process it, live it and share it. In Jesus' name I pray, amen.

What is God speaking to you? What action will you take in light of today's devotion?

#DontDoLifeAloneDevo #ReadPrayApplyRemain

Genesis 8-10, Psalms 4:1-8, Proverbs 1:20-23, Matthew 4:12-25

January 5

"Let your light so shine before men, that they may see your good works and glorify your Father in heaven." Matthew 5:16

Every day we are given opportunities to make an impact in people's lives. What a privilege it is to follow Jesus. Let's use our life to point people to the One who changed everything for us.

Thank you God for another day and for your word. Help me process it, live it and share it. In Jesus' name I pray, amen.

What is God speaking to you? What action will you take in light of today's devotion?

#DontDoLifeAloneDevo #ReadPrayApplyRemain

Genesis 11:1-13:4, Psalms 5:1-12, Proverbs 1:24-28, Matthew 5:1-26

January 6

"And whoever compels you to go one mile, go with him two." Matthew 5:41

Some people are good at the status quo, but there is always going to be an opportunity to go beyond that. Love well, serve more, and forgive quickly. The second mile is rarely crowded.

Thank you God for another day and for your word. Help me process it, live it and share it. In Jesus' name I pray, amen.

What is God speaking to you? What action will you take in light of today's devotion?

#DontDoLifeAloneDevo #ReadPrayApplyRemain

Genesis 13:5-15:21, Psalms 6:1-10, Proverbs 1:29-33, Matthew 5:27-48

January 7

"Give us this day our daily bread." Matthew 6:11

It's easy to reach out to God when we have an emergency, but do we trust Him to provide for our daily needs? Do we even acknowledge that He is our provider?

Thank you God for another day and for your word. Help me process it, live it and share it. In Jesus' name I pray, amen.

What is God speaking to you? What action will you take in light of today's devotion?

#DontDoLifeAloneDevo #ReadPrayApplyRemain

Genesis 16-18:15, Psalms 7:1-17, Proverbs 2:1-5, Matthew 6:1-24

January 8

"He stores up sound wisdom for the upright; He is a shield to those who walk uprightly."
Proverbs 2:7

You don't have to defend yourself. Sometimes life puts us in defense mode, but if we will keep our eyes on Jesus and live in a way that is pleasing to Him, He will take care of the situation and us.

Thank you God for another day and for your word. Help me process it, live it and share it. In Jesus' name I pray, amen.

What is God speaking to you? What action will you take in light of today's devotion?

#DontDoLifeAloneDevo #ReadPrayApplyRemain

Genesis 18:16-19:38, Psalms 8:1-9, Proverbs 2:6-15, Matthew 6:25-7:14

January 9

"I will praise You, O LORD, with my whole heart; I will tell of all Your marvelous works." Psalms 9:1

It can be easy to focus on your problems and forget to say thank you for what God has already done. Don't allow what's wrong with you to keep you from praising what's right about God and His faithfulness in your life.

Thank you God for another day and for your word. Help me process it, live it and share it. In Jesus' name I pray, amen.

What is God speaking to you? What action will you take in light of today's devotion?

#DontDoLifeAloneDevo #ReadPrayApplyRemain

Genesis 20-22, Psalms 9:1-12, Proverbs 2:16-22, Matthew 7:15-29

January 10

"In all your ways acknowledge Him, and He shall direct your paths." Proverbs 3:6

If you are a follower of Jesus, of course you want Him to direct your paths; but are you willing to acknowledge Him in all of your ways first? God is faithful. Seek Him first and watch this verse come to life.

Thank you God for another day and for your word. Help me process it, live it and share it. In Jesus' name I pray, amen.

What is God speaking to you? What action will you take in light of today's devotion?

#DontDoLifeAloneDevo #ReadPrayApplyRemain

Genesis 23:1-24:51, Psalms 9:13-20, Proverbs 3:1-6, Matthew 8:1-17

January 11

"But Jacob said, 'Sell me your birthright as of this day.'" Genesis 25:31

Esau came home hungry and Jacob just happened to be making some food. Esau got so worked up over how he felt, that he was willing to trade his birthright (inheritance) for one bowl of soup. What seems good may not be God's best for your life. Don't settle.

Thank you God for another day and for your word. Help me process it, live it and share it. In Jesus' name I pray, amen.

What is God speaking to you? What action will you take in light of today's devotion?

#DontDoLifeAloneDevo #ReadPrayApplyRemain

Genesis 24:52-26:16, Psalms 10:1-15, Proverbs 3:7-8, Matthew 8:18-34

January 12

"No one puts a piece of unshrunk cloth on an old garment; for the patch pulls away from the garment, and the tear is made worse." Matthew 9:16

Sometimes you have to stop trying to fix the old pair of pants and replace them. Stop trying to fix the thing that God is trying to replace in your life. Jesus makes all things new. Trust Him.

Thank you God for another day and for your word. Help me process it, live it and share it. In Jesus' name I pray, amen.

What is God speaking to you? What action will you take in light of today's devotion?

#DontDoLifeAloneDevo #ReadPrayApplyRemain

Genesis 26:17-27:46, Psalms 10:16-18, Proverbs 3:9-10, Matthew 9:1-17

January 13

"For whom the LORD loves He corrects, just as a father the son in whom he delights." Proverbs 3:12

Correction is not always easy to receive, but when we walk in humility and choose to stay teachable, anything is possible. The process is not always easy, but it will be worth it.

Thank you God for another day and for your word. Help me process it, live it and share it. In Jesus' name I pray, amen.

What is God speaking to you? What action will you take in light of today's devotion?

#DontDoLifeAloneDevo #ReadPrayApplyRema

Genesis 28:1-29:35, Psalms 11:1-7, Proverbs 3:11-12, Matthew 9:18-38

January 14

"I am the God of Bethel, where you anointed
the pillar and where you made a vow to Me.
Now arise, get out of this land, and return to the
land of your family." Genesis 31:13

It's great to be forward thinking, but sometimes
we have to go back and reflect on what God has
already done in our life in order to take our next
step.

Thank you God for another day and for your
word. Help me process it, live it and share it. In
sus' name I pray, amen.

's God speaking to you? What action will
in light of today's devotion?

AloneDevo #ReadPrayApplyRemain

:16, Psalms 12:1-8, Proverbs
10:1-23

January 15

"Are not two sparrows sold for a copper coin? And not one of them falls to the ground apart from your Father's will." Matthew 10:29

It can be easy to go through a situation and forget about God's ability to redeem what we are going through. Every time you see a bird flying, remember this verse. God is more mindful of you than you realize.

Thank you God for another day and for your word. Help me process it, live it and share it. In Jesus' name I pray, amen.

What is God speaking to you? What action will you take in light of today's devotion?

#DontDoLifeAloneDevo #ReadPrayApplyRemain

Genesis 31:17-32:12, Psalms 13:1-6, Proverbs 3:16-18, Matthew 10:24-11:6

January 16

"And He said, 'Let Me go, for the day breaks.'
But he said, 'I will not let You go unless You
bless me!'" Genesis 32:26

Jacob wrestled with God until He blessed him.
Sometimes we give up right before we
experience a breakthrough. Whatever you are
praying for, keep praying.

Thank you God for another day and for your
word. Help me process it, live it and share it. In
Jesus' name I pray, amen.

What is God speaking to you? What action will
you take in light of today's devotion?

#DontDoLifeAloneDevo #ReadPrayApplyRemain

Genesis 32:13-34:31, Psalms 14:1-7, Proverbs
3:19-20, Matthew 11:7-30

January 17

"And in His name Gentiles will trust." Matthew 12:21

From a biblical and cultural standpoint Gentiles were anyone that was not from a Jewish descent, but spiritually, Gentiles did not follow the God of the Jews. Jesus is hope and He levels the playing field. Thankfully, Jesus is someone that everybody can put his or her trust in, and He's ready when we are.

Thank you God for another day and for your word. Help me process it, live it and share it. In Jesus' name I pray, amen.

What is God speaking to you? What action will you take in light of today's devotion?

#DontDoLifeAloneDevo #ReadPrayApplyRemain

Genesis 35:1-36:43, Psalms 15:1-5, Proverbs 3:21-26, Matthew 12:1-21

January 18

"Now Joseph had a dream, and he told it to his brothers; and they hated him even more."
Genesis 37:5

If you read the story of Joseph you know his brothers always had issues with him. That being said, we are all going to have opposition when it comes to our dreams. Even when somebody hates your dream, be encouraged and dream on. If God gave it to you, God will see you through.

Thank you God for another day and for your word. Help me process it, live it and share it. In Jesus' name I pray, amen.

What is God speaking to you? What action will you take in light of today's devotion?

#DontDoLifeAloneDevo #ReadPrayApplyRemain

Genesis 37:1-38:30, Psalms 16:1-11, Proverbs 3:27-32, Matthew 12:22-45

January 19

"He who has ears to hear, let him hear!"
Matthew 13:9

When Jesus talked about having ears to hear,
He did not just mean hearing something
audibly. You can hear something but not actually
listen and apply it. What is the Lord speaking to
you?

Thank you God for another day and for your
word. Help me process it, live it and share it. In
Jesus' name I pray, amen.

What is God speaking to you? What action will
you take in light of today's devotion?

#DontDoLifeAloneDevo #ReadPrayApplyRemain

Genesis 39:1-41:16, Psalms 17:1-15, Proverbs
3:33-35, Matthew 12:46-13:23

January 20

"The LORD is my rock and my fortress and my deliverer; My God, my strength, in whom I will trust; My shield and the horn of my salvation, my stronghold." Psalms 18:2

Some people have family or friends that they can call when things get tough, but God is available for everyone. It's good to have someone to lean on, but it's even better to have a God that will cover you. And you do!

Thank you God for another day and for your word. Help me process it, live it and share it. In Jesus' name I pray, amen.

What is God speaking to you? What action will you take in light of today's devotion?

#DontDoLifeAloneDevo #ReadPrayApplyRemain

Genesis 41:17-42:17, Psalms 18:1-15, Proverbs 4:1-6, Matthew 13:24-13:46

January 21

"He sent from above, He took me; He drew me out of many waters." Psalms 18:16

We don't always realize it, but there have been many circumstances that should have taken us out, but they didn't. They didn't because God pulled us out when the waters of life started to drown us. God is faithful.

Thank you God for another day and for your word. Help me process it, live it and share it. In Jesus' name I pray, amen.

What is God speaking to you? What action will you take in light of today's devotion?

#DontDoLifeAloneDevo #ReadPrayApplyRemain

Genesis 42:18-43:34, Psalms 18:16-36, Proverbs 4:7-10, Matthew 13:47-14:12

January 22

"But Jesus said to them, 'They do not need to go away. You give them something to eat.'"
Matthew 14:16

In the Gospels we read that on many occasions Jesus met physical needs before ministering to spiritual needs. Don't miss out on an opportunity to bless someone today and be a tangible expression of God's love.

Thank you God for another day and for your word. Help me process it, live it and share it. In Jesus' name I pray, amen.

What is God speaking to you? What action will you take in light of today's devotion?

#DontDoLifeAloneDevo #ReadPrayApplyRemain

Genesis 44:1-45:28, Psalms 18:37-50, Proverbs 4:11-13, Matthew 14:13-36

January 23

"The heavens declare the glory of God; And the firmament shows His handiwork." Psalms 19:1

One way to connect with God is to take a minute to appreciate the beauty of creation. Daily He paints us a sky that is constantly changing. Don't miss out on the beauty that God gives us to enjoy every day.

Thank you God for another day and for your word. Help me process it, live it and share it. In Jesus' name I pray, amen.

What is God speaking to you? What action will you take in light of today's devotion?

#DontDoLifeAloneDevo #ReadPrayApplyRemain

Genesis 46:1-47:31, Psalms 19:1-14, Proverbs 4:14-19, Matthew 15:1-28

January 24

"Keep your heart with all diligence, for out of it spring the issues of life." Proverbs 4:23

We need to be mindful of who and what we allow to speak into our lives. Hurt people can hurt people, but healthy people can help bring healing to others. Don't allow your heart to grow bitter or cold.

Thank you God for another day and for your word. Help me process it, live it and share it. In Jesus' name I pray, amen.

What is God speaking to you? What action will you take in light of today's devotion?

#DontDoLifeAloneDevo #ReadPrayApplyRemain

Genesis 48:1-49:33, Psalms 20:1-9, Proverbs 4:20-27, Matthew 15:29-39

January 25

"But as for you, you meant evil against me; but God meant it for good, in order to bring it about as it is this day, to save many people alive."
Genesis 50:20

God has the ability to redeem any situation in order to fulfill His purpose. Even when you find yourself going through a difficult circumstance, remember that God is still working in your favor.

Thank you God for another day and for your word. Help me process it, live it and share it. In Jesus' name I pray, amen.

What is God speaking to you? What action will you take in light of today's devotion?

#DontDoLifeAloneDevo #ReadPrayApplyRemain

Genesis 50:1-Exodus 2:10, Psalms 21:1-13, Proverbs 5:1-6, Matthew 16:13-17:9

January 26

"So when the LORD saw that he turned aside to look, God called to him from the midst of the bush and said, 'Moses, Moses!' And he said, 'Here I am.'" Exodus 3:4

God spoke to Moses through a burning bush, but that only happened one time. God may want to speak to you in a different way today than He did yesterday. Open your heart up to receive all that God has for you.

Thank you God for another day and for your word. Help me process it, live it and share it. In Jesus' name I pray, amen.

What is God speaking to you? What action will you take in light of today's devotion?

#DontDoLifeAloneDevo #ReadPrayApplyRemain

Exodus 2:11-3:22, Psalms 22:1-18, Proverbs 5:7-14, Matthew 17:10-27

January 27

"Moreover if your brother sins against you, go and tell him his fault between you and him alone. If he hears you, you have gained your brother." Matthew 18:15

We are going to have conflict with people, but the Bible instructs us on how to handle it. When you have an issue, confront it. Sometimes hard conversations are necessary for growth.

Thank you God for another day and for your word. Help me process it, live it and share it. In Jesus' name I pray, amen.

What is God speaking to you? What action will you take in light of today's devotion?

#DontDoLifeAloneDevo #ReadPrayApplyRemain

Exodus 4:1-5:21, Psalms 22:19-31, Proverbs 5:15-21, Matthew 18:1-20

January 28

"He restores my soul; He leads me in the paths of righteousness For His name's sake." Psalms 23:3

God does not just want you to survive the day; He wants to fill you back up. It does not matter how tired, frustrated, or hurt you may be, make room for God to move in your life today. Spending time with God like you are doing right now, is a great start.

Thank you God for another day and for your word. Help me process it, live it and share it. In Jesus' name I pray, amen.

What is God speaking to you? What action will you take in light of today's devotion?

#DontDoLifeAloneDevo #ReadPrayApplyRemain

Exodus 5:22-7:25, Psalms 23:1-6, Proverbs 5:22-23, Matthew 18:21-19:12

January 29

"Jesus said to him, 'If you want to be perfect, go, sell what you have and give to the poor, and you will have treasure in heaven; and come, follow Me.'" Matthew 19:21

For the rich young ruler, his identity was found in his possessions. Money and things won't bring you fulfillment. Titles and other people's opinions won't bring you fulfillment. What's holding you back?

Thank you God for another day and for your word. Help me process it, live it and share it. In Jesus' name I pray, amen.

What is God speaking to you? What action will you take in light of today's devotion?

#DontDoLifeAloneDevo #ReadPrayApplyRemain

Exodus 8:1-9:35, Psalms 24:1-10, Proverbs 6:1-5, Matthew 19:13-30

January 30

"Lead me in Your truth and teach me, for You are the God of my salvation; On You I wait all the day." Psalms 25:5

We all want to be successful, but are we allowing God's word to lead the way? Information is so accessible but without wisdom and proper application it is worthless. Check your source and keep growing.

Thank you God for another day and for your word. Help me process it, live it and share it. In Jesus' name I pray, amen.

What is God speaking to you? What action will you take in light of today's devotion?

#DontDoLifeAloneDevo #ReadPrayApplyRemain

Exodus 10:1-12:13, Psalms 25:1-15, Proverbs 6:6-11, Matthew 20:1-28

January 31

"And seeing a fig tree by the road, He came to it and found nothing on it but leaves, and said to it, 'Let no fruit grow on you ever again.' Immediately the fig tree withered away."
Matthew 21:19

Is your life producing good fruit? Sometimes we allow being busy to get in the way of doing what God has created us for. Ask God to show you how you are doing and make an adjustment if it's needed.

Thank you God for another day and for your word. Help me process it, live it and share it. In Jesus' name I pray, amen.

What is God speaking to you? What action will you take in light of today's devotion?

#DontDoLifeAloneDevo #ReadPrayApplyRemain

Exodus 12:14-13:16, Psalms 25:16-22. Proverbs 6:12-15, Matthew 20:29-21:22

February 1

"And the LORD went before them by day in a pillar of cloud to lead the way, and by night in a pillar of fire to give them light, so as to go by day and night." Exodus 13:21

God can lead us however He chooses, but are we following? Maybe you are praying for direction, but you are struggling to find it. Instead of focusing on finding direction, focus on seeking Jesus. He will lead you.

Thank you God for another day and for your word. Help me process it, live it and share it. In Jesus' name I pray, amen.

What is God speaking to you? What action will you take in light of today's devotion?

#DontDoLifeAloneDevo #ReadPrayApplyRemain

Exodus 13:17-15:18, Psalms 26:1-12, Proverbs 6:16-19, Matthew 21:23-46

February 2

"My son, keep your father's command, and do not forsake the law of your mother." Proverbs 6:20

God puts people in our life to help us reach our full potential and make the most of the opportunities that we are given. If you get wisdom from someone, hold on to it. Grab a pen and piece of paper and write it down. Don't miss out on an opportunity to grow.

Thank you God for another day and for your word. Help me process it, live it and share it. In Jesus' name I pray, amen.

What is God speaking to you? What action will you take in light of today's devotion?

#DontDoLifeAloneDevo #ReadPrayApplyRemain

Exodus 15:19-17:7, Psalms 27:1-6, Proverbs 6:20-26, Matthew 22:1-33

February 3

"But Moses' hands became heavy; so they took a stone and put it under him, and he sat on it. And Aaron and Hur supported his hands, one on one side, and the other on the other side; and his hands were steady until the going down of the sun." Exodus 17:12

As long as the arms of Moses stayed up, they were winning the battle. Thankfully, Moses had Aaron and Hur to come alongside of him to hold his arms up when he got tired. Do you have anyone to hold you up when you grow weary? If not, it's time to find them.

Thank you God for another day and for your word. Help me process it, live it and share it. In Jesus' name I pray, amen.

What is God speaking to you? What action will you take in light of today's devotion?

#DontDoLifeAloneDevo #ReadPrayApplyRemain

Exodus 17:8-19:15, Psalms 27:7-14, Proverbs 6:27-35, Matthew 22:34-23:12

February 4

"Remember the Sabbath day, to keep it holy."
Exodus 20:8

God knows us better than we know ourselves.
From a physical standpoint God does not need
to rest. However, He instituted the Sabbath to
make sure that we take time to rest and reflect
on all that He has done for us. Working hard is a
great thing, but so is rest. Don't disregard the
Sabbath.

Thank you God for another day and for your
word. Help me process it, live it and share it. In
Jesus' name I pray, amen.

What is God speaking to you? What action will
you take in light of today's devotion?

#DontDoLifeAloneDevo #ReadPrayApplyRemain

Exodus 19:16-21:21, Psalms 28:1-9, Proverbs
7:1-5, Matthew 23:13-39

February 5

"You shall not follow a crowd to do evil; nor shall you testify in a dispute so as to turn aside after many to pervert justice." Exodus 23:2

Who is influencing your life? For better or for worse, the people that we have in our life have an effect on us. Proverbs 15:22 reminds us that there is wisdom in a multitude of counselors, just be mindful of who they are.

Thank you God for another day and for your word. Help me process it, live it and share it. In Jesus' name I pray, amen.

What is God speaking to you? What action will you take in light of today's devotion?

#DontDoLifeAloneDevo #ReadPrayApplyRemain

Exodus 21:22-23:13, Psalms 29:1-11, Proverbs 7:6-23, Matthew 24:1-28

February 6

"You have turned for me my mourning into dancing; You have put off my sackcloth and clothed me with gladness." Psalms 30:11

God faithfully walks with us in the good and bad times. The best part though, God has the ability to change the outcome of our situation. Remember to give Him praise when you are going through the valley and on the other side of it.

Thank you God for another day and for your word. Help me process it, live it and share it. In Jesus' name I pray, amen.

What is God speaking to you? What action will you take in light of today's devotion?

#DontDoLifeAloneDevo #ReadPrayApplyRemain

Exodus 23:14-25:40, Psalms 30:1-12, Proverbs 7:24-27, Matthew 24:29-51

February 7

"And a cubit on one side and a cubit on the other side, of what remains of the length of the curtains of the tent, shall hang over the sides of the tabernacle, on this side and on that side, to cover it." Exodus 26:13

In Exodus 26, God gives very specific instructions on how to build the tabernacle. Sometimes God shares the details and sometimes we have to walk by faith. Regardless of how much information you receive, God has you covered. Trust Him.

Thank you God for another day and for your word. Help me process it, live it and share it. In Jesus' name I pray, amen.

What is God speaking to you? What action will you take in light of today's devotion?

#DontDoLifeAloneDevo #ReadPrayApplyRemain

Exodus 26:1-27:21, Psalms 31:1-8, Proverbs 8:1-11, Matthew 25:1-30

February 8

"And the King will answer and say to them, 'Assuredly, I say to you, inasmuch as you did it to one of the least of these My brethren, you did it to Me.'" Matthew 25:40

Who can you bless today? Of course we want to be a blessing to our family or friends, but Jesus encourages us to also be a blessing to those that others may write off. Don't miss out on an opportunity to be a tangible expression of the love of God today.

Thank you God for another day and for your word. Help me process it, live it and share it. In Jesus' name I pray, amen.

What is God speaking to you? What action will you take in light of today's devotion?

#DontDoLifeAloneDevo #ReadPrayApplyRemain

Exodus 28:1-43, Psalms 31:9-18, Proverbs 8:12-13, Matthew 25:31-26:13

February 9

"Be of good courage, and He shall strengthen your heart, all you who hope in the LORD."
Psalms 31:24

This verse is a great reminder of who our source is. We can go through life with courage regardless of what we may face, because God is where our hope comes from.

Thank you God for another day and for your word. Help me process it, live it and share it. In Jesus' name I pray, amen.

What is God speaking to you? What action will you take in light of today's devotion?

#DontDoLifeAloneDevo #ReadPrayApplyRemain

Exodus 29:1-30:10, Psalms 31:19-24, Proverbs 8:14-26, Matthew 26:14-46

February 10

"But Jesus kept silent. And the high priest answered and said to Him, 'I put You under oath by the living God: Tell us if You are the Christ, the Son of God!'" Matthew 26:63

How often do we try to justify ourselves to people that have no intentions of actually hearing us? Jesus chose to keep silent because He knew that He was doing what His Heavenly Father told Him to do. If you are right in God's eyes, let the Lord run defense for you.

Thank you God for another day and for your word. Help me process it, live it and share it. In Jesus' name I pray, amen.

What is God speaking to you? What action will you take in light of today's devotion?

#DontDoLifeAloneDevo #ReadPrayApplyRemain

Exodus 30:11-31:18, Psalms 32:1-11, Proverbs 8:27-32, Matthew 26:47-68

February 11

"So the LORD spoke to Moses face to face, as a man speaks to his friend. And he would return to the camp, but his servant Joshua the son of Nun, a young man, did not depart from the tabernacle." Exodus 33:11

Joshua helped Moses as he led the nation of Israel, but he also got a front row seat to see how Moses interacted with God. We all have to get to a place where we can embrace God for ourselves. Don't be afraid to stay and seek God when others have left the building.

Thank you God for another day and for your word. Help me process it, live it and share it. In Jesus' name I pray, amen.

What is God speaking to you? What action will you take in light of today's devotion?

#DontDoLifeAloneDevo #ReadPrayApplyRemain

Exodus 32:1-33:23, Psalms 33:1-11, Proverbs 8:33-36, Matthew 26:69-27:14

February 12

"Let Your mercy, O LORD, be upon us, just as we hope in You." Psalms 33:22

We are not always consistent with our devotion to God, but His mercy is always available for us. The word mercy shows up in the Bible over 140 times. Receive it today and remember to extend the same level of mercy to others that God has given to you.

Thank you God for another day and for your word. Help me process it, live it and share it. In Jesus' name I pray, amen.

What is God speaking to you? What action will you take in light of today's devotion?

#DontDoLifeAloneDevo #ReadPrayApplyRemain

Exodus 34:1-35:9, Psalms 33:12-22, Proverbs 9:1-6, Matthew 27:15-31

February 13

"I will bless the LORD at all times; His praise shall continually be in my mouth." Psalms 34:1

Some days we are on the mountain top and some days we are in the valley. Regardless of where we find ourselves, we have a choice to make. We get to decide how we are going to respond. I will bless the Lord at all times. He got me here. He will see me through.

Thank you God for another day and for your word. Help me process it, live it and share it. In Jesus' name I pray, amen.

What is God speaking to you? What action will you take in light of today's devotion?

#DontDoLifeAloneDevo #ReadPrayApplyRemain

Exodus 35:10-36:38, Psalms 34:1-10, Proverbs 9:7-8, Matthew 27:32-66

February 14

"He is not here; for He is risen, as He said.
Come, see the place where the Lord lay."
Matthew 28:6

Some days feel impossible, but with God
nothing is impossible. Because Jesus got up, we
can too! Walk in the victory that Jesus lived,
died, and rose again to give you. Easter is one
day a year, but we can celebrate His resurrection
every day.

Thank you God for another day and for your
word. Help me process it, live it and share it. In
Jesus' name I pray, amen.

What is God speaking to you? What action will
you take in light of today's devotion?

#DontDoLifeAloneDevo #ReadPrayApplyRemain

Exodus 37:1-38:31, Psalms 34:11-22, Proverbs
9:9-10, Matthew 28:1-20

February 15

"Then Jesus said to them, 'Follow Me, and I will make you become fishers of men.'" Mark 1:17

When Jesus said, "Follow Me," it was more then just an invitation. It was a commitment to lead and give the disciples purpose. He offers us the same invitation today. Have you responded yet?

Thank you God for another day and for your word. Help me process it, live it and share it. In Jesus' name I pray, amen.

What is God speaking to you? What action will you take in light of today's devotion?

#DontDoLifeAloneDevo #ReadPrayApplyRemain

Exodus 39:1-40:38, Psalms 35:1-16, Proverbs 9:11-12, Mark 1:1-28

February 16

"Now in the morning, having risen a long while before daylight, He went out and departed to a solitary place; and there He prayed." Mark 1:35

If Jesus made time to go pray and spend time with His heavenly Father, how much more should we? If we are not intentional, communication with God will become an occasional occurrence. Pray first and God will help you take care of the rest.

Thank you God for another day and for your word. Help me process it, live it and share it. In Jesus' name I pray, amen.

What is God speaking to you? What action will you take in light of today's devotion?

#DontDoLifeAloneDevo #ReadPrayApplyRemain

Leviticus 1:1-3:17, Psalms 35:17-28, Proverbs 9:13-18, Mark 1:29-2:12

February 17

"When Jesus heard it, He said to them, 'Those who are well have no need of a physician, but those who are sick. I did not come to call the righteous, but sinners, to repentance.'" Mark 2:17

Jesus loves us. He allows us to come as we are, but He loves us to much to leave us like that. Don't forget where God has brought you from. Don't forget that He is still trying to reach those who are lost.

Thank you God for another day and for your word. Help me process it, live it and share it. In Jesus' name I pray, amen.

What is God speaking to you? What action will you take in light of today's devotion?

#DontDoLifeAloneDevo #ReadPrayApplyRemain

Leviticus 4:1-5:19, Psalms 36:1-12, Proverbs 10:1-2, Mark 2:13-3:6

February 18

"A fire shall always be burning on the altar; it shall never go out." Leviticus 6:13

In the tabernacle, someone had to make sure that the fire never went out. In our relationship with God and in our relationships with others, we have to own that responsibility. It's not always easy, but the investment is worth it.

Thank you God for another day and for your word. Help me process it, live it and share it. In Jesus' name I pray, amen.

What is God speaking to you? What action will you take in light of today's devotion?

#DontDoLifeAloneDevo #ReadPrayApplyRemain

Leviticus 6:1-7:27, Psalms 37:1-11, Proverbs 10:3-4, Mark 3:7-30

February 19

"And He said to them, 'He who has ears to hear, let him hear!'" Mark 4:9

Just because there are things being said, it does not mean that we are listening. Don't miss out on an opportunity to hear and respond to what the Holy Spirit is trying to speak into your life today.

Thank you God for another day and for your word. Help me process it, live it and share it. In Jesus' name I pray, amen.

What is God speaking to you? What action will you take in light of today's devotion?

#DontDoLifeAloneDevo #ReadPrayApplyRemain

Leviticus 7:28-8:36, Psalms 37:12-29, Proverbs 10:5, Mark 3:31-4:25

February 20

"Then He arose and rebuked the wind, and said to the sea, 'Peace, be still!' And the wind ceased and there was a great calm." Mark 4:39

The disciples that were on the boat with Jesus were upset because He was sleeping during the storm. Storms do not intimidate Jesus. After they woke Him up, Jesus calmed the storm. Sometimes He calms the storms and sometimes Jesus rides them out with us. The best part is that Jesus is on the boat regardless.

Thank you God for another day and for your word. Help me process it, live it and share it. In Jesus' name I pray, amen.

What is God speaking to you? What action will you take in light of today's devotion?

#DontDoLifeAloneDevo #ReadPrayApplyRemain

Leviticus 9:7-10:20, Psalms 37:30-40, Proverbs 10:6-7, Mark 4:26-5:20

February 21

"He who walks with integrity walks securely, but he who perverts his ways will become known." Proverbs 10:9

Peace of mind makes all the difference in the world. God already knows who we really are, so there is no need to hide behind a mask. If you need help, ask for it. If you messed up, confess and ask for forgiveness. Walk in integrity and be free in Jesus' name.

Thank you God for another day and for your word. Help me process it, live it and share it. In Jesus' name I pray, amen.

What is God speaking to you? What action will you take in light of today's devotion?

#DontDoLifeAloneDevo #ReadPrayApplyRemain

Leviticus 11:1-12:8, Psalms 38:1-22, Proverbs 10:8-9, Mark 5:21-43

February 22

"LORD, make me to know my end, and what is the measure of my days, that I may know how frail I am." Psalms 39:4

Every single day that we are given is a blessing, but sometimes we don't live like that. Our life is a gift and we should live accordingly. Not only should we be intentional with our own life, we need to do the same with our relationships.

Thank you God for another day and for your word. Help me process it, live it and share it. In Jesus' name I pray, amen.

What is God speaking to you? What action will you take in light of today's devotion?

#DontDoLifeAloneDevo #ReadPrayApplyRemain

Leviticus 13:1-59, Psalms 39:1-13, Proverbs 10:10, Mark 6:1-29

February 23

"And when He had sent them away, He departed to the mountain to pray." Mark 6:46

We are encouraged to stay busy in the culture that we live in. Once Jesus kicked off His ministry, everybody wanted His attention. Even though there was always plenty of need, Jesus found time to pray. If Jesus, the Son of God, spent time in prayer with His heavenly Father, how much more should we?

Thank you God for another day and for your word. Help me process it, live it and share it. In Jesus' name I pray, amen.

What is God speaking to you? What action will you take in light of today's devotion?

#DontDoLifeAloneDevo #ReadPrayApplyRemain

Leviticus 14:1-57, Psalms 40:1-10, Proverbs 10:11-12, Mark 6:30-56

February 24

"Wise people store up knowledge, but the mouth of the foolish is near destruction." Proverbs 10:14

No matter how much we think we know; there is always someone who knows more. God's word reminds us that His ways are higher than our ways. Pay attention, find wisdom, and take notes. None of us have arrived and we all have room to grow.

Thank you God for another day and for your word. Help me process it, live it and share it. In Jesus' name I pray, amen.

What is God speaking to you? What action will you take in light of today's devotion?

#DontDoLifeAloneDevo #ReadPrayApplyRemain

Leviticus 15:1-16:28, Psalms 40:11-17, Proverbs 10:13-14, Mark 7:1-23

February 25

"Blessed is he who considers the poor; the LORD will deliver him in time of trouble." Psalms 41:1

Jesus wants us to care about what He cares about. God loves everyone, but sometimes we can overlook people. It is easy to get so focused on trying to take care of ourselves that we miss other people that are struggling. God blesses us to be a blessing and when we do something for the least of these, we are doing it unto the Lord.

Thank you God for another day and for your word. Help me process it, live it and share it. In Jesus' name I pray, amen.

What is God speaking to you? What action will you take in light of today's devotion?

#DontDoLifeAloneDevo #ReadPrayApplyRemain

Leviticus 16:29-18:30, Psalms 41:1-13, Proverbs 10:15-16, Mark 7:24-8:10

February 26

"For what will it profit a man if he gains the whole world, and loses his own soul?" Mark 8:36

We work hard for a lot of things. Some people work hard to take care of their family and some to build wealth. Some people work hard to gain influence and some to get approval. It's not bad to work hard, but don't lose what matters most in the process. Jesus is most concerned with your soul. Focus on Jesus first and let Him handle the rest.

Thank you God for another day and for your word. Help me process it, live it and share it. In Jesus' name I pray, amen.

What is God speaking to you? What action will you take in light of today's devotion?

#DontDoLifeAloneDevo #ReadPrayApplyRemain

Leviticus 19:1-20:21, Psalms 42:1-11, Proverbs 10:17, Mark 8:11-38

February 27

"Why are you cast down, O my soul? And why are you disquieted within me? Hope in God; for I shall yet praise Him, the help of my countenance and my God." Psalms 43:5

Our situations are not always good and sometimes we are going to get discouraged. We can't always change our circumstances, but we can change how we respond. We can choose to put our hope in the Lord. Instead of focusing on what's wrong with us, we can praise the Lord for all that He has done. Be encouraged friend!

Thank you God for another day and for your word. Help me process it, live it and share it. In Jesus' name I pray, amen.

What is God speaking to you? What action will you take in light of today's devotion?

#DontDoLifeAloneDevo #ReadPrayApplyRemain

Leviticus 20:22-22:16, Psalms 43:1-5, Proverbs 10:18, Mark 9:1-29

February 28

"And He sat down, called the twelve, and said to them, 'If anyone desires to be first, he shall be last of all and servant of all.'" Mark 9:35

The greatest title that we could ever hold, next to being a son or daughter of God, is servant. It's not the most popular position in our world, but it is in God's eyes. Jesus showed us how to serve. If you want to be great, love and serve others well.

Thank you God for another day and for your word. Help me process it, live it and share it. In Jesus' name I pray, amen.

What is God speaking to you? What action will you take in light of today's devotion?

#DontDoLifeAloneDevo #ReadPrayApplyRemain

Leviticus 22:17-23:44, Psalms 44:1-8, Proverbs 10:19, Mark 9:30-10:12

March 1

"The lips of the righteous feed many, but fools die for lack of wisdom." Proverbs 10:21

The words that we use are powerful. Our words can be used to do harm or to do something good. Don't miss an opportunity to speak life and encourage someone today. Your words could change the direction of their entire week for the better.

Thank you God for another day and for your word. Help me process it, live it and share it. In Jesus' name I pray, amen.

What is God speaking to you? What action will you take in light of today's devotion?

#DontDoLifeAloneDevo #ReadPrayApplyRemain

Leviticus 24:1-25:46, Psalms 44:9-26, Proverbs 10:20-21, Mark 10:13-31

March 2

"The blessing of the LORD makes one rich, and He adds no sorrow with it." Proverbs 10:22

When most people hear or read the word rich, financial wealth may come to mind first. However there are things that have a greater value than the balance in our bank account. At the end of the day, your definition of a rich life will be apparent by the way that you live. Live in a way that is pleasing to the Lord and He will teach you how to experience a rich life.

Thank you God for another day and for your word. Help me process it, live it and share it. In Jesus' name I pray, amen.

What is God speaking to you? What action will you take in light of today's devotion?

#DontDoLifeAloneDevo #ReadPrayApplyRemain

Leviticus 25:47-27:13, Psalms 45:1-17, Proverbs 10:22, Mark 10:32-52

March 3

"Be still, and know that I am God; I will be exalted among the nations, I will be exalted in the earth!" Psalms 46:10

God is always working, but we don't always notice. Sometimes we are not aware because we are distracted with other things. Whether you are facing a difficult situation right now or if things could not be better, take some time to be still. God is working on your behalf.

Thank you God for another day and for your word. Help me process it, live it and share it. In Jesus' name I pray, amen.

What is God speaking to you? What action will you take in light of today's devotion?

#DontDoLifeAloneDevo #ReadPrayApplyRemain

Leviticus 27:14-34, Numbers 1:1-54, Psalms 46:1-11, Proverbs 10:23, Mark 11:1-26

March 4

"When the whirlwind passes by, the wicked is no more, but the righteous have an everlasting foundation." Proverbs 10:25

This verse starts out by saying, "when the whirlwind passes by." Storms are going to come, but God is faithful. Storms are not easy to endure, but God is greater than any storm that life will bring. Be encouraged and hold on to Jesus.

Thank you God for another day and for your word. Help me process it, live it and share it. In Jesus' name I pray, amen.

What is God speaking to you? What action will you take in light of today's devotion?

#DontDoLifeAloneDevo #ReadPrayApplyRemain

Numbers 2:1-3:51, Psalms 47:1-9, Proverbs 10:24-25, Mark 11:26-12:17

March 5

"'And you shall love the LORD your God with all your heart, with all your soul, with all your mind, and with all your strength.' This is the first commandment." Mark 12:30

God does not just want you to know about Him, God wants you to know Him. A relationship with God is about way more than just going to church once a week. Because of Jesus we don't have to do life alone. Don't miss out on experiencing a growing relationship with Jesus.

Thank you God for another day and for your word. Help me process it, live it and share it. In Jesus' name I pray, amen.

What is God speaking to you? What action will you take in light of today's devotion?

#DontDoLifeAloneDevo #ReadPrayApplyRemain

Numbers 4:1-5:31, Psalms 48:1-14, Proverbs 10:26, Mark 12:18-37

March 6

"But when you are arrested and stand trial, don't worry in advance about what to say. Just say what God tells you at that time, for it is not you who will be speaking, but the Holy Spirit."
Mark 13:11

Jesus never promised that life would be easy, but He did promise that He would always be with us. Regardless of what you may be facing, allow God to use you in the situation. He will give you the words to say when the time is right.

Thank you God for another day and for your word. Help me process it, live it and share it. In Jesus' name I pray, amen.

What is God speaking to you? What action will you take in light of today's devotion?

#DontDoLifeAloneDevo #ReadPrayApplyRemain

Numbers 6:1-7:89, Psalms 49:1-20, Proverbs 10:27-28, Mark 12:38-13:13

March 7

"Offer to God thanksgiving, and pay your vows to the Most High." Psalms 50:14

Regardless of what we are going through, the Lord is worthy of our praise. No matter what we may face today, we have plenty of reasons to be thankful. Gratitude changes everything. Don't forget to say thank you.

Thank you God for another day and for your word. Help me process it, live it and share it. In Jesus' name I pray, amen.

What is God speaking to you? What action will you take in light of today's devotion?

#DontDoLifeAloneDevo #ReadPrayApplyRemain

Numbers 8:1-9:23, Psalms 50:1-23, Proverbs 10:29-30, Mark 13:14-37

March 8

"Create in me a clean heart, O God, and renew a steadfast spirit within me." Psalms 51:10

The Bible reminds us that God can make all things new. Sometimes you just have to hit reset. Don't be afraid to begin again. If you are still breathing, God is not finished with your story.

Thank you God for another day and for your word. Help me process it, live it and share it. In Jesus' name I pray, amen.

What is God speaking to you? What action will you take in light of today's devotion?

#DontDoLifeAloneDevo #ReadPrayApplyRemain

Numbers 10:1-11:23, Psalms 51:1-19, Proverbs 10:31-32, Mark 14:1-21

March 9

"And He said, 'Abba, Father, all things are possible for You. Take this cup away from Me; nevertheless, not what I will, but what You will. '"
Mark 14:36

Preparing to go to the cross was not an easy thing to process, but Jesus did not run away from it. He made time to seek the Father in prayer and then He submitted to God's will. Being obedient is not always going to be easy, but it will always be worth it. His obedience changed everything for us.

Thank you God for another day and for your word. Help me process it, live it and share it. In Jesus' name I pray, amen.

What is God speaking to you? What action will you take in light of today's devotion?

#DontDoLifeAloneDevo #ReadPrayApplyRemain

Numbers 11:24-13:33, Psalms 52:1-9, Proverbs 11:1-3, Mark 14:22-52

March 10

"God looks down from heaven upon the children of men, to see if there are any who understand, who seek God." Psalms 53:2

You don't have to be the most talented person in the world or have superpowers to be used by God. We tend to focus a lot on trivial things, but God looks at our heart. If you are humble and obedient, God can and will use you to make an impact in the world. Enjoy the journey!

Thank you God for another day and for your word. Help me process it, live it and share it. In Jesus' name I pray, amen.

What is God speaking to you? What action will you take in light of today's devotion?

#DontDoLifeAloneDevo #ReadPrayApplyRemain

Numbers 14:1-15:16, Psalms 53:1-6, Proverbs 11:4, Mark 14:53-72

March 11

"Then the veil of the temple was torn in two from top to bottom." Mark 15:38

Before Jesus went to the cross for us a priest would have to go to the temple and make a sacrifice for our sins. Jesus was the ultimate sacrifice and He willingly gave His life up for us. The only barrier between us and God are the things that we allow to get in the way. He is only one prayer away.

Thank you God for another day and for your word. Help me process it, live it and share it. In Jesus' name I pray, amen.

What is God speaking to you? What action will you take in light of today's devotion?

#DontDoLifeAloneDevo #ReadPrayApplyRemain

Numbers 15:17-16:40, Psalms 54:1-7, Proverbs 11:5-6, Mark 15:1-47

March 12

"And He said to them, "Go into all the world and preach the gospel to every creature." Mark 16:15

The news and media are usually filled with everything but good news, but there is something worth talking about. The word gospel literally means good news. Everybody needs hope and Jesus is the source. Once you have hope, you need to share it.

Thank you God for another day and for your word. Help me process it, live it and share it. In Jesus' name I pray, amen.

What is God speaking to you? What action will you take in light of today's devotion?

#DontDoLifeAloneDevo #ReadPrayApplyRemain

Numbers 16:41-18:32, Psalms 55:1-23, Proverbs 11:7, Mark 16:1-20

March 13

"So it was, that while he was serving as priest before God in the order of his division," Luke 1:8

This verse hardly seems noteworthy but there is more to it than meets the eye. Zacharias and his wife Elizabeth had been praying and seeking the Lord for a miracle. This verse records what a normal workday looked like for Zacharias, but the day did not end as usual. God showed up in the midst of a normal day and changed their life forever! Stay faithful and watch God show up when you least expect it.

Thank you God for another day and for your word. Help me process it, live it and share it. In Jesus' name I pray, amen.

What is God speaking to you? What action will you take in light of today's devotion?

#DontDoLifeAloneDevo #ReadPrayApplyRemain

Numbers 19:1-20:29, Psalms 56:1-13, Proverbs 11:8, Luke 1:1-25

March 14

"By the blessing of the upright the city is exalted, but it is overthrown by the mouth of the wicked." Proverbs 11:11

God can use you to make a difference in your world. You have an opportunity to share Jesus with your family, your friends, and your community that others don't. Make the most of it.

Thank you God for another day and for your word. Help me process it, live it and share it. In Jesus' name I pray, amen.

What is God speaking to you? What action will you take in light of today's devotion?

#DontDoLifeAloneDevo #ReadPrayApplyRemain

Numbers 21:1-22:20, Psalms 57:1-11, Proverbs 11:9-11, Luke 1:26-56

March 15

"Then the LORD opened the mouth of the donkey, and she said to Balaam, 'What have I done to you, that you have struck me these three times?'" Numbers 22:28

In this verse, we see that God spoke through a donkey. The truth is, God is able to speak through anything, at any point in time. The Lord may want to speak to you in an unconventional way. Be ready to receive whatever He has to share with you today.

Thank you God for another day and for your word. Help me process it, live it and share it. In Jesus' name I pray, amen.

What is God speaking to you? What action will you take in light of today's devotion?

#DontDoLifeAloneDevo #ReadPrayApplyRemain

Numbers 22:21-23:30, Psalms 58:1-11, Proverbs 11:12-13, Luke 1:57-80

March 16

"Where there is no counsel, the people fall; But in the multitude of counselors there is safety." Proverbs 11:14

Time and time again, the Bible speaks to the value of good relationships. God never intended for us to do life alone. We need people speaking good things into our life. If you have those people, appreciate them and if you don't, seek them out.

Thank you God for another day and for your word. Help me process it, live it and share it. In Jesus' name I pray, amen.

What is God speaking to you? What action will you take in light of today's devotion?

#DontDoLifeAloneDevo #ReadPrayApplyRemain

Numbers 24:1-25:18, Psalms 59:1-17, Proverbs 11:14, Luke 2:1-35

March 17

"And Jesus increased in wisdom and stature, and in favor with God and men." Luke 2:52

Jesus grew in every area of His life in a healthy way. It's great to be physically healthy, but we should be growing in wisdom, in obedience, and in our relationships with God and others too. What can you do intentionally to grow today?

Thank you God for another day and for your word. Help me process it, live it and share it. In Jesus' name I pray, amen.

What is God speaking to you? What action will you take in light of today's devotion?

#DontDoLifeAloneDevo #ReadPrayApplyRemain

Numbers 26:1-51 Psalms, 60:1-12, Proverbs 11:15, Luke 2:36-52

March 18

"He answered and said to them, 'He who has two tunics, let him give to him who has none; and he who has food, let him do likewise.'" Luke 3:11

The Lord is good to us. God will provide for our needs, but He will also give us an opportunity to do the same for someone else. Don't forget that we are blessed to be a blessing.

Thank you God for another day and for your word. Help me process it, live it and share it. In Jesus' name I pray, amen.

What is God speaking to you? What action will you take in light of today's devotion?

#DontDoLifeAloneDevo #ReadPrayApplyRemain

Numbers 26:52-28:15, Psalms 61:1-8, Proverbs 11:16-17, Luke 3:1-22

March 19

"He only is my rock and my salvation; He is my defense; I shall not be greatly moved." Psalms 62:2

Where does your hope come from? When everything else falls apart, where do you turn? The psalmist reminds us that God is our source of strength. We can be tempted to turn to other things, but there is only one that will never let us down and that is Jesus. Lean into Him today.

Thank you God for another day and for your word. Help me process it, live it and share it. In Jesus' name I pray, amen.

What is God speaking to you? What action will you take in light of today's devotion?

#DontDoLifeAloneDevo #ReadPrayApplyRemain

Numbers 28:16-29:40, Psalms 62:1-12, Proverbs 11:18-19, Luke 3:23-38

March 20

"Then Jesus, being filled with the Holy Spirit, returned from the Jordan and was led by the Spirit into the wilderness" Luke 4:1

Jesus did not stumble into the wilderness. This verse says that the Holy Spirit led Him there. Sometimes God will lead us through less than ideal places in order to get us where He needs us to go. When you find yourself in the wilderness, focus on Jesus and keep going. God is still at work.

Thank you God for another day and for your word. Help me process it, live it and share it. In Jesus' name I pray, amen.

What is God speaking to you? What action will you take in light of today's devotion?

#DontDoLifeAloneDevo #ReadPrayApplyRemain

Numbers 30:1-31:54, Psalms 63:1-11, Proverbs 11:20-21, Luke 4:1-30

March 21

"When He had stopped speaking, He said to Simon, 'Launch out into the deep and let down your nets for a catch.'" Luke 5:4

When Jesus gave this instruction, He was not talking to rookie fisherman. These guys knew what they were doing and they had not caught any fish that day. God is really good at what He does. Regardless of what we think we know, when we are obedient the outcome is on the Lord. His best for our life is always better than our plans.

Thank you God for another day and for your word. Help me process it, live it and share it. In Jesus' name I pray, amen.

What is God speaking to you? What action will you take in light of today's devotion?

#DontDoLifeAloneDevo #ReadPrayApplyRemain

Numbers 32:1-33:39, Psalms 64:1-10, Proverbs 11:22, Luke 4:31-5:11

March 22

"And when they could not find how they might bring him in, because of the crowd, they went up on the housetop and let him down with his bed through the tiling into the midst before Jesus." Luke 5:19

Some people have friends that are there when things are convenient, but real friends show up when things get tough. Don't take your relationships for granted. You never know when you may need someone to carry you.

Thank you God for another day and for your word. Help me process it, live it and share it. In Jesus' name I pray, amen.

What is God speaking to you? What action will you take in light of today's devotion?

#DontDoLifeAloneDevo #ReadPrayApplyRemain

Numbers 33:40-35:34, Psalms 65:1-13, Proverbs 11:23, Luke 5:12-28

March 23

"Jesus answered and said to them, 'Those who are well have no need of a physician, but those who are sick.'" Luke 5:31

Some people think that they need to get themselves together before they turn to the Lord, but it is actually quite the opposite. We will never find healing and restoration without Jesus involved in the process. Let God minister to you today regardless of your need or how far off track you may be. He is ready when you are.

Thank you God for another day and for your word. Help me process it, live it and share it. In Jesus' name I pray, amen.

What is God speaking to you? What action will you take in light of today's devotion?

#DontDoLifeAloneDevo #ReadPrayApplyRemain

Numbers 36:1-Deuteronomy 1:46, Psalms 66:1-20, Proverbs 11:24-26, Luke 5:29-6:11

March 24

"You must not fear them, for the LORD your God Himself fights for you." Deuteronomy 3:22

Regardless of where you have been or what you may be facing, God has your back. He is cheering for you. God will fight for you. You don't have to live in fear or defeat when God is on your side. Trust Him today!

Thank you God for another day and for your word. Help me process it, live it and share it. In Jesus' name I pray, amen.

What is God speaking to you? What action will you take in light of today's devotion?

#DontDoLifeAloneDevo #ReadPrayApplyRemain

Deuteronomy 2:1-3:29, Psalms 67:1-7, Proverbs 11:27, Luke 6:12-38

March 25

"Only take heed to yourself, and diligently keep yourself, lest you forget the things your eyes have seen, and lest they depart from your heart all the days of your life. And teach them to your children and your grandchildren" Deuteronomy 4:9

In the Old Testament we see that altars were created to be a reminder of what God had done. They were not only good for the people that had an encounter with God to be reminded, but for others to be encouraged along the way. Don't forget what God has already done and share those stories.

Thank you God for another day and for your word. Help me process it, live it and share it. In Jesus' name I pray, amen.

What is God speaking to you? What action will you take in light of today's devotion?

#DontDoLifeAloneDevo #ReadPrayApplyRemain

Deuteronomy 4:1-49, Psalms 68:1-18, Proverbs 11:28, Luke 6:39-7:10

March 26

"You shall walk in all the ways which the LORD your God has commanded you, that you may live and that it may be well with you, and that you may prolong your days in the land which you shall possess." Deuteronomy 5:33

There are going to be times in life where you feel like giving up or going in a different direction, but God is saying to stay the course. Sometimes we give up right before we get to experience what God has for us. Trust Him and keep going. You won't regret it.

Thank you God for another day and for your word. Help me process it, live it and share it. In Jesus' name I pray, amen.

What is God speaking to you? What action will you take in light of today's devotion?

#DontDoLifeAloneDevo #ReadPrayApplyRemain

Deuteronomy 5:1-6:25, Psalms 68:19-35, Proverbs 11:29-31, Luke 7:11-35

March 27

"When you have eaten and are full, then you shall bless the LORD your God for the good land which He has given you." Deuteronomy 8:10

Don't forget to say thank you! We can get so used to our blessings that we forget that they are blessings. God is faithful to provide all that we need, but remember to acknowledge Him for how good He has been to you. Gratitude changes everything.

Thank you God for another day and for your word. Help me process it, live it and share it. In Jesus' name I pray, amen.

What is God speaking to you? What action will you take in light of today's devotion?

#DontDoLifeAloneDevo #ReadPrayApplyRemain

Deuteronomy 7:1-8:20, Psalms 69:1-18, Proverbs 12:1, Luke 7:36-8:3

March 28

"The humble will see their God at work and be glad. Let all who seek God's help be encouraged." Psalms 69:32

We can get so caught up in the business of life that we can miss the most important things. God is working on your behalf even when you don't recognize Him. God is more mindful of you today than you realize. Be encouraged!

Thank you God for another day and for your word. Help me process it, live it and share it. In Jesus' name I pray, amen.

What is God speaking to you? What action will you take in light of today's devotion?

#DontDoLifeAloneDevo #ReadPrayApplyRemain

Deuteronomy 9:1-10:22, Psalms 69:19-36, Proverbs 12:2-3, Luke 8:4-21

March 29

"'Return to your own house, and tell what great things God has done for you.' And he went his way and proclaimed throughout the whole city what great things Jesus had done for him." Luke 8:39

We are quick to share a great dinner experience or a great movie. However, we can neglect to share the amazing things that the Lord has done and is doing in our lives. The Bible says that the redeemed of the Lord should say so. Don't forget to testify about the goodness of God in your life.

Thank you God for another day and for your word. Help me process it, live it and share it. In Jesus' name I pray, amen.

What is God speaking to you? What action will you take in light of today's devotion?

#DontDoLifeAloneDevo #ReadPrayApplyRemain

Deuteronomy 11:1-12:32, Psalms 70:1-5, Proverbs 12:4, Luke 8:22-39

March 30

"And He said to her, 'Daughter, be of good cheer; your faith has made you well. Go in peace.'" Luke 8:48

The woman with the issue of blood had tried every other option, but then Jesus showed up. God can change the situation that has been troubling you for years in a matter of seconds. God can use people and situations to help us, but ultimately God is our source and He wants to move in your life today.

Thank you God for another day and for your word. Help me process it, live it and share it. In Jesus' name I pray, amen.

What is God speaking to you? What action will you take in light of today's devotion?

#DontDoLifeAloneDevo #ReadPrayApplyRemain

Deuteronomy 13:1-15:23, Psalms 71:1-24, Proverbs 12:5-7, Luke 8:40-9:6

March 31

"For what profit is it to a man if he gains the whole world, and is himself destroyed or lost?" Luke 9:25

It's good to be mindful of how you are doing physically or financially, but what about your soul? We can get so caught up in trying to survive that we neglect the most important things. The greatest gain that can happen in your life today is to know God more.

Thank you God for another day and for your word. Help me process it, live it and share it. In Jesus' name I pray, amen.

What is God speaking to you? What action will you take in light of today's devotion?

#DontDoLifeAloneDevo #ReadPrayApplyRemain

Deuteronomy 16:1-17:20, Psalms 72:1-20, Proverbs 12:8-9, Luke 9:7-27

April 1

"My flesh and my heart fail; but God is the strength of my heart and my portion forever." Psalms 73:26

The chorus of the hymn "The Solid Rock" says, "On Christ, the solid rock I stand, all other ground is sinking sand." How true those lyrics are. And when everything is falling apart, God won't. You will not regret putting your trust in Jesus.

Thank you God for another day and for your word. Help me process it, live it and share it. In Jesus' name I pray, amen.

What is God speaking to you? What action will you take in light of today's devotion?

#DontDoLifeAloneDevo #ReadPrayApplyRemain

Deuteronomy 18:1-20:20, Psalms 73:1-28, Proverbs 12:10, Luke 9:28-50

April 2

"Now it happened as they journeyed on the road, that someone said to Him, 'Lord, I will follow You wherever You go.'" Luke 9:57

Jesus had a lot of people tell Him that they wanted to follow Him but for many they let other things get in the way. Of course there are things that we have to take care of, but don't let your "but first" stop you from responding to the greatest invitation that any of us will ever receive - to follow Jesus.

Thank you God for another day and for your word. Help me process it, live it and share it. In Jesus' name I pray, amen.

What is God speaking to you? What action will you take in light of today's devotion?

#DontDoLifeAloneDevo #ReadPrayApplyRemain

Deuteronomy 21:1-22:30, Psalms 74:1-23, Proverbs 12:11, Luke 9:51-10:12

April 3

"For I tell you that many prophets and kings have desired to see what you see, and have not seen it, and to hear what you hear, and have not heard it. " Luke 10:24

It's possible to have your eyes wide open and still miss something. Sometimes we hear things but are not actually paying attention to be able to process what we are hearing. God wants to speak and show you things today. Even in the midst of what you assume to be a normal day, God could share something amazing with you. Look for Him.

Thank you God for another day and for your word. Help me process it, live it and share it. In Jesus' name I pray, amen.

What is God speaking to you? What action will you take in light of today's devotion?

#DontDoLifeAloneDevo #ReadPrayApplyRemain

Deuteronomy 23:1-25:19,, Psalms 75:1-10, Proverbs 12:12-14, Luke 10:13-37

April 4

"But one thing is needed, and Mary has chosen that good part, which will not be taken away from her." Luke 10:42

When Jesus showed up, Martha stayed busy taking care of things while Mary focused on Jesus. Sure there were things that needed to be done, but Martha was missing out on an opportunity to enjoy the presence of Jesus. Our relationships matter the most. Don't miss out on an opportunity to be present.

Thank you God for another day and for your word. Help me process it, live it and share it. In Jesus' name I pray, amen.

What is God speaking to you? What action will you take in light of today's devotion?

#DontDoLifeAloneDevo #ReadPrayApplyRemain

Deuteronomy 26:1-27:26, Psalms 76:1-12, Proverbs 12:15-17, Luke 10:38-11:13

April 5

"Blessed shall you be when you come in, and blessed shall you be when you go out."
Deuteronomy 28:6

Jesus said if we love Him we will walk in obedience. Some people look at obedience as a burden, but it's actually a privilege. When I think about how good God has been to me and the fact that He first loved me, it's a no brainer. God's plans are better than ours and His blessings are worth our obedience.

Thank you God for another day and for your word. Help me process it, live it and share it. In Jesus' name I pray, amen.

What is God speaking to you? What action will you take in light of today's devotion?

#DontDoLifeAloneDevo #ReadPrayApplyRemain

Deuteronomy 28:1-68, Psalms 77:1-20, Proverbs 12:18, Luke 11:14-36

April 6

"See, I have set before you today life and good, death and evil." Deuteronomy 30:15

Sometimes we make decisions not realizing the weight behind them. Sometimes we don't acknowledge things that are going on and in our indecision we are actually making a decision. God always brings life to the table. Whatever He has for you, it's going to be your best option every time. Choose life!

Thank you God for another day and for your word. Help me process it, live it and share it. In Jesus' name I pray, amen.

What is God speaking to you? What action will you take in light of today's devotion?

#DontDoLifeAloneDevo #ReadPrayApplyRemain

Deuteronomy 29:1-30:20, Psalms 78:1-31, Proverbs 12:19-20, Luke 11:37-12:7

April 7

"For where your treasure is, there your heart will be also." Luke 12:34

You invest in what ever it is that you value the most. The Lord has blessed us with resources and opportunities. Every new day brings new possibilities. How are you investing your time, talent, and treasure? If your investments do not reflect your values, it's time for a change.

Thank you God for another day and for your word. Help me process it, live it and share it. In Jesus' name I pray, amen.

What is God speaking to you? What action will you take in light of today's devotion?

#DontDoLifeAloneDevo #ReadPrayApplyRemain

Deuteronomy 31:1-32:27, Psalms 78:32-55, Proverbs 12:21-23, Luke 12:8-34

April 8

"The hand of the diligent will rule, but the lazy man will be put to forced labor." Proverbs 12:24

So many people want something to change in their life, but they are not willing to do anything about it. God is ready to meet you at your point of need, but you have to meet Him there too. Commit whatever you are doing to the Lord and He will bless you and give you the strength to excel beyond anything that you could do on your own.

Thank you God for another day and for your word. Help me process it, live it and share it. In Jesus' name I pray, amen.

What is God speaking to you? What action will you take in light of today's devotion?

#DontDoLifeAloneDevo #ReadPrayApplyRemain

Deuteronomy 32:28-52, Psalms 78:56-64, Proverbs 12:24, Luke 12:35-59

April 9

"Anxiety in the heart of man causes depression, but a good word makes it glad." Proverbs 12:25

Our words can make a huge impact for better or for worse. If you focus on your circumstances, it may lead you to worry. Don't take for granted the good words that have been spoken over you. Don't miss out on an opportunity to share life-giving words with someone else today.

Thank you God for another day and for your word. Help me process it, live it and share it. In Jesus' name I pray, amen.

What is God speaking to you? What action will you take in light of today's devotion?

#DontDoLifeAloneDevo #ReadPrayApplyRemain

Deuteronomy 33:1-29, Psalms 78:65-72, Proverbs 12:25, Luke 13:1-21

April 10

"Have I not commanded you? Be strong and of good courage; do not be afraid, nor be dismayed, for the LORD your God is with you wherever you go." Joshua 1:9

As Joshua is preparing to take over as the leader of Israel God tells him three times to be strong and of good courage. God repeats himself on purpose. He is trying to give Joshua a new soundtrack for his life. God wants to give you a new soundtrack too. Be strong and of good courage, friend. Embrace His words today.

Thank you God for another day and for your word. Help me process it, live it and share it. In Jesus' name I pray, amen.

What is God speaking to you? What action will you take in light of today's devotion?

#DontDoLifeAloneDevo #ReadPrayApplyRemain

Deuteronomy 34, Joshua 1:1-2:24, Psalms 79:1-13, Proverbs 12:26, Luke 13:22-14:6

April 11

"And Joshua said to the people, 'Sanctify yourselves, for tomorrow the LORD will do wonders among you.'" Joshua 3:5

How you begin a new day sometimes determines what you get out of it. When you come into a situation expecting something great to happen, you won't miss it when it does. Gratitude helps you recognize what God has already done, but faith causes you to thank Him before you get there. You never know what God may have in store.

Thank you God for another day and for your word. Help me process it, live it and share it. In Jesus' name I pray, amen.

What is God speaking to you? What action will you take in light of today's devotion?

#DontDoLifeAloneDevo #ReadPrayApplyRemain

Joshua 3:1-4:24, Psalms 80:1-19, Proverbs 12:27-28, Luke 14:7-35

April 12

"Then all the tax collectors and the sinners drew near to Him to hear Him." Luke 15:1

People wanted to be with Jesus. Some religious people had an issue with Jesus spending so much time with sinners, but that did not deter Him. Jesus loves people where they are and He speaks hope into their life. If you want to model your life after anyone, be like Jesus.

Thank you God for another day and for your word. Help me process it, live it and share it. In Jesus' name I pray, amen.

What is God speaking to you? What action will you take in light of today's devotion?

#DontDoLifeAloneDevo #ReadPrayApplyRemain

Joshua 5:1-7:15, Psalms 81:1-16, Proverbs 13:1, Luke 15:1-32

April 13

"He who is faithful in what is least is faithful also in much; and he who is unjust in what is least is unjust also in much." Luke 16:10

Sometimes, we want more. The question is, how are we doing with what we have? You may want or need more money, but like an old song says if you don't manage it well, "mo money mo problems." God gives us the opportunity to be stewards of our lives and the way we manage our time, relationships, talent, and resources really matters.

Thank you God for another day and for your word. Help me process it, live it and share it. In Jesus' name I pray, amen.

What is God speaking to you? What action will you take in light of today's devotion?

#DontDoLifeAloneDevo #ReadPrayApplyRemain

Joshua 7:16-9:2, Psalms 82:1-8, Proverbs 13:2-3, Luke 16:1-18

April 14

"And the apostles said to the Lord, 'Increase our faith.'" Luke 17:5

The apostles got to see Jesus in action and in the flesh almost every day and they still wanted their faith to increase. There is no limit to what God can do. Seek Him more and embrace all that He has for you today.

Thank you God for another day and for your word. Help me process it, live it and share it. In Jesus' name I pray, amen.

What is God speaking to you? What action will you take in light of today's devotion?

#DontDoLifeAloneDevo #ReadPrayApplyRemain

Joshua 9:3-10:43, Psalms 83:1-18, Proverbs 13:4, Luke 16:19-17:10

April 15

"And one of them, when he saw that he was healed, returned, and with a loud voice glorified God" Luke 17:15

This passage points out that Jesus healed ten lepers but only one of them came back to say thank you. In the next verse it says that he was a Samaritan. In other words, he did not have any prior relationship with God. God has been so good to us and it's easy to take God's blessings for granted. Don't forget to give thanks and glory to God for all that He has done for you.

Thank you God for another day and for your word. Help me process it, live it and share it. In Jesus' name I pray, amen.

What is God speaking to you? What action will you take in light of today's devotion?

#DontDoLifeAloneDevo #ReadPrayApplyRemain

Joshua 11:1-12:24, Psalms 84:1-12, Proverbs 13:5-6, Luke 17:11-37

April 16

"Then He spoke a parable to them, that men always ought to pray and not lose heart" Luke 18:1

Sometimes we give up right before we experience a breakthrough in our lives. When we pray by faith we are surrendering our situation into God's hands. God is good at what He does. Prayer changes things. Don't lose heart.

Thank you God for another day and for your word. Help me process it, live it and share it. In Jesus' name I pray, amen.

What is God speaking to you? What action will you take in light of today's devotion?

#DontDoLifeAloneDevo #ReadPrayApplyRemain

Joshua 13:1-14:15, Psalms 85:1-13, Proverbs 13:7-8, Luke 18:1-17

April 17

"By pride comes nothing but strife, but with the well-advised is wisdom." Proverbs 13:10

Nobody likes to be hindered but sometimes we get in our own way. Pride can keep us from experiencing God's best for our life. You will never be able to overdose on wisdom. Don't be afraid to ask for help. God is faithful.

Thank you God for another day and for your word. Help me process it, live it and share it. In Jesus' name I pray, amen.

What is God speaking to you? What action will you take in light of today's devotion?

#DontDoLifeAloneDevo #ReadPrayApplyRemain

Joshua 15:1-63, Psalms 86:1-17, Proverbs 13:9-10, Luke 18:18-43

April 18

"For the Son of Man has come to seek and to save that which was lost." Luke 19:10

Jesus has done a lot of incredible things, but His focus has never changed. Jesus came to find His lost kids. If your kids were lost, you would do whatever it took to find them. The world is looking for hope and Jesus is the source.

Thank you God for another day and for your word. Help me process it, live it and share it. In Jesus' name I pray, amen.

What is God speaking to you? What action will you take in light of today's devotion?

#DontDoLifeAloneDevo #ReadPrayApplyRemain

Joshua 16:1-18:28, Psalms 87:1-7, Proverbs 13:11, Luke 19:1-27

April 19

"Hope deferred makes the heart sick, but when the desire comes, it is a tree of life." Proverbs 13:12

How many times have you been at the end of your self with a situation and then God showed up? One of the reasons that it is good to stay in God's word and in prayer is to remind ourselves about the hope that we have in the Lord! With God involved, hope is always on the table.

Thank you God for another day and for your word. Help me process it, live it and share it. In Jesus' name I pray, amen.

What is God speaking to you? What action will you take in light of today's devotion?

#DontDoLifeAloneDevo #ReadPrayApplyRemain

Joshua 19:1-20:9, Psalms 88:1-18, Proverbs 13:12-14, Luke 19:28-48

April 20

"I will sing of the mercies of the LORD forever;
With my mouth will I make known Your
faithfulness to all generations." Psalms 89:1

Have you shared about God's faithfulness
recently? The Bible reminds us that the
redeemed of the Lord should say so. God has
been so good to us! Share a testimony and tell
the world about our incredible God.

Thank you God for another day and for your
word. Help me process it, live it and share it. In
Jesus' name I pray, amen.

What is God speaking to you? What action will
you take in light of today's devotion?

#DontDoLifeAloneDevo #ReadPrayApplyRemain

Joshua 21:1-22:20, Psalms 89:1-13, Proverbs
13:15-16, Luke 20:1-26

April 21

"A wicked messenger falls into trouble, but a faithful ambassador brings health." Proverbs 13:17

Every time we open our mouth, we have an opportunity to make an impact. You decide what kind of impact that you want to make. There are plenty of people speaking death. Speak life and bring health.

Thank you God for another day and for your word. Help me process it, live it and share it. In Jesus' name I pray, amen.

What is God speaking to you? What action will you take in light of today's devotion?

#DontDoLifeAloneDevo #ReadPrayApplyRemain

Joshua 22:21-23:16, Psalms 89:14-37, Proverbs 13:17-19, Luke 20:27-47

April 22

"He who walks with wise men will be wise, but the companion of fools will be destroyed." Proverbs 13:20

Our relationships make all of the difference in the world. A rich life has nothing to do with money. Be mindful of who you are walking with. If you want to enjoy the journey, don't do life alone.

Thank you God for another day and for your word. Help me process it, live it and share it. In Jesus' name I pray, amen.

What is God speaking to you? What action will you take in light of today's devotion?

#DontDoLifeAloneDevo #ReadPrayApplyRemain

Joshua 24:1-33, Psalms 89:38-52, Proverbs 13:20-23, Luke 21:1-28

April 23

"He who dwells in the secret place of the Most High shall abide under the shadow of the Almighty." Psalms 91:1

There is nothing wrong with taking a few minutes to clear your mind or have a conversation with a friend, but true peace is found in God's presence. Stop trying to navigate your life on your own. Seek the Lord today and let Him give you rest.

Thank you God for another day and for your word. Help me process it, live it and share it. In Jesus' name I pray, amen.

What is God speaking to you? What action will you take in light of today's devotion?

#DontDoLifeAloneDevo #ReadPrayApplyRemain

Judges 1:1-2:9, Psalms 90:1-91:16, Proverbs 13:24-25, Luke 21:29-22:13

April 24

"When all that generation had been gathered to their fathers, another generation arose after them who did not know the LORD nor the work which He had done for Israel." Judges 2:10

A whole generation not knowing the Lord was not an instant thing. It is not hard for your priorities to change and for you to start heading in the wrong direction. Never forget what God has done and never forget to tell others about Him.

Thank you God for another day and for your word. Help me process it, live it and share it. In Jesus' name I pray, amen.

What is God speaking to you? What action will you take in light of today's devotion?

#DontDoLifeAloneDevo #ReadPrayApplyRemain

Judges 2:10-3:31, Psalms 92:1-93:5, Proverbs 14:1-2, Luke 22:14-34

April 25

"Father, if it is Your will, take this cup away from Me; nevertheless not My will, but Yours, be done." Luke 22:42

Going to the cross was no easy task, but Jesus chose to submit how He felt in the moment for God's will when He said nevertheless. Being obedient is not always easy, but walking by faith and following God will always be worth it.

Thank you God for another day and for your word. Help me process it, live it and share it. In Jesus' name I pray, amen.

What is God speaking to you? What action will you take in light of today's devotion?

#DontDoLifeAloneDevo #ReadPrayApplyRemain

Judges 4:1-5:31, Psalms 94:1-23, Proverbs 14:3-4, Luke 22:35-53

April 26

"Let us come before His presence with thanksgiving; Let us shout joyfully to Him with psalms." Psalms 95:2

It is never a bad time to give God praise. God wants us to bring our needs to Him, but don't forget to give Him glory for what He has already done. Today instead of focusing on your needs or problems, take some time to focus on the One that has carried you through even the most difficult seasons of life.

Thank you God for another day and for your word. Help me process it, live it and share it. In Jesus' name I pray, amen.

What is God speaking to you? What action will you take in light of today's devotion?

#DontDoLifeAloneDevo #ReadPrayApplyRemain

Judges 6:1-40, Psalms 95:1-96:13, Proverbs 14:5-6, Luke 22:54-23:12

April 27

"And the LORD said to Gideon, 'The people who are with you are too many for Me to give the Midianites into their hands, lest Israel claim glory for itself against Me, saying, 'My own hand has saved me.'" Judges 7:2

Regardless of what you may be facing, when God is involved in your life, you are always in the majority. Sometimes our situations remind us who our source is, but that's not a bad thing. Trust God even when it does not make sense.

Thank you God for another day and for your word. Help me process it, live it and share it. In Jesus' name I pray, amen.

What is God speaking to you? What action will you take in light of today's devotion?

#DontDoLifeAloneDevo #ReadPrayApplyRemain

Judges 7:1-8:17, Psalms 97:1-98:9, Proverbs 14:7-8, Luke 23:13-43

April 28

"Then they went in and did not find the body of the Lord Jesus." Luke 24:3

Our hope is not rooted in a good story about a good guy. Our hope is rooted in the truth that Jesus came, died, and then rose on the third day. He conquered death, hell, and the grave and because He lives we can too.

Thank you God for another day and for your word. Help me process it, live it and share it. In Jesus' name I pray, amen.

What is God speaking to you? What action will you take in light of today's devotion?

#DontDoLifeAloneDevo #ReadPrayApplyRemain

Judges 8:18-9:21, Psalms 99:1-9, Proverbs 14:9-10, Luke 23:44-24:12

April 29

"There is a way that seems right to a man, but its end is the way of death." Proverbs 14:12

Sometimes we question how or why God does things, but history proves that we do not have it all figured out. Don't lean solely on your own understanding. God is good at what He does. Trust Him.

Thank you God for another day and for your word. Help me process it, live it and share it. In Jesus' name I pray, amen.

What is God speaking to you? What action will you take in light of today's devotion?

#DontDoLifeAloneDevo #ReadPrayApplyRemain

Judges 9:22-10:18, Psalms 100:1-5, Proverbs 14:11-12, Luke 24:13-53

April 30

"And the Word became flesh and dwelt among us, and we beheld His glory, the glory as of the only begotten of the Father, full of grace and truth." John 1:14

When Jesus showed up, things changed. He wants to do the same thing through us. We are the hands and feet of Jesus. Let Him use you where you are today.

Thank you God for another day and for your word. Help me process it, live it and share it. In Jesus' name I pray, amen.

What is God speaking to you? What action will you take in light of today's devotion?

#DontDoLifeAloneDevo #ReadPrayApplyRemain

Judges 11:1-12:15, Psalms 101:1-8, Proverbs 14:13-14, John 1:1-28

May 1

"A wise man fears and departs from evil, but a fool rages and is self-confident." Proverbs 14:16

As a child my mom told me to keep my hands off of the stove. I thought she was keeping me from something good but she knew that she was keeping me from burning my hands. Depart from evil. What God has for you is way better than anything the world has to offer.

Thank you God for another day and for your word. Help me process it, live it and share it. In Jesus' name I pray, amen.

What is God speaking to you? What action will you take in light of today's devotion?

#DontDoLifeAloneDevo #ReadPrayApplyRemain

Judges 13:1-14:20, Psalms 102:1-28, Proverbs 14:15-16, John 1:29-1:51

May 2

"Bless the LORD, O my soul, and forget not all His benefits." Psalms 103:2

There are so many blessings that come from being in a relationship with God. The only way that we can experience all that He has for us is to continue to know, seek and trust Him. Jesus loves you so much.

Thank you God for another day and for your word. Help me process it, live it and share it. In Jesus' name I pray, amen.

What is God speaking to you? What action will you take in light of today's devotion?

#DontDoLifeAloneDevo #ReadPrayApplyRemain

Judges 15:1-16:31, Psalms 103:1-22, Proverbs 14:17-19, John 2:1-2:25

May 3

"For God so loved the world that He gave His only begotten Son, that whoever believes in Him should not perish but have everlasting life." John 3:16

God's focus has never changed. Jesus came, lived, died and rose again to offer His love, hope and salvation to the world and we get to be a part of sharing that story.

Thank you God for another day and for your word. Help me process it, live it and share it. In Jesus' name I pray, amen.

What is God speaking to you? What action will you take in light of today's devotion?

#DontDoLifeAloneDevo #ReadPrayApplyRemain

Judges 17:1-18:31, Psalms 104:1-23, Proverbs 14:20-21, John 3:1-3:21

May 4

"He must increase, but I must decrease." John 3:30

When you magnify something everything else gets smaller. Instead of focusing on your problems focus on the problem solver. As He increases and we decrease, things will come into proper perspective.

Thank you God for another day and for your word. Help me process it, live it and share it. In Jesus' name I pray, amen.

What is God speaking to you? What action will you take in light of today's devotion?

#DontDoLifeAloneDevo #ReadPrayApplyRemain

Judges 19:1-20:48, Psalms 104:24-35, Proverbs 14:22-24, John 3:22-4:3

May 5

"But whoever drinks of the water that I shall give him will never thirst. But the water that I shall give him will become in him a fountain of water springing up into everlasting life." John 4:14

There are so many sources that over promise but under deliver. Jesus is the only well that we can tap into that will never run dry. Stop trying to quench your thirst with broken wells.

Thank you God for another day and for your word. Help me process it, live it and share it. In Jesus' name I pray, amen.

What is God speaking to you? What action will you take in light of today's devotion?

#DontDoLifeAloneDevo #ReadPrayApplyRemain

Judges 21:1-22, Psalms 105:1-15, Proverbs 14:25, John 4:4-42

May 6

"For Jesus Himself testified that a prophet has no honor in his own country." John 4:44

You may not always have support from the places that you expected it to come from, but God has your back and that is more than enough. Don't focus on who is against you, but be thankful for who is for you.

Thank you God for another day and for your word. Help me process it, live it and share it. In Jesus' name I pray, amen.

What is God speaking to you? What action will you take in light of today's devotion?

#DontDoLifeAloneDevo #ReadPrayApplyRemain

Ruth 2:1-4:22, Psalms 105:16-36, Proverbs 14:26-27, John 4:43-54

May 7

"He who is slow to wrath has great understanding, but he who is impulsive exalts folly." Proverbs 14:29

There is nothing wrong with processing something before you respond. Most mistakes are made impulsively. Take time to pray and let God lead the way.

Thank you God for another day and for your word. Help me process it, live it and share it. In Jesus' name I pray, amen.

What is God speaking to you? What action will you take in light of today's devotion?

#DontDoLifeAloneDevo #ReadPrayApplyRemain

1 Samuel 1:1-2:21, Psalms 105:37-45, Proverbs 14:28-29, John 5:1-23

May 8

"A sound heart is life to the body, but envy is rottenness to the bones." Proverbs 14:30

There is nothing wrong with having goals or passion, but we have to learn to rest. Striving for more all of the time will leave you empty. A rich life has more to do with the condition of your heart then your net worth. Check your heart.

Thank you God for another day and for your word. Help me process it, live it and share it. In Jesus' name I pray, amen.

What is God speaking to you? What action will you take in light of today's devotion?

#DontDoLifeAloneDevo #ReadPrayApplyRemain

1 Samuel 2:22-4:22, Psalms 106:1-12, Proverbs 14:30-31, John 5:24-47

May 9

"They forgot God their Savior, who had done great things in Egypt." Psalms 106:21

In the Old Testament we see on many occasions that stone altars were built to help people remember what God had done. You may not need to gather a pile of rocks, but it is never a bad thing to revisit testimonies of God's faithfulness for some encouragement.

Thank you God for another day and for your word. Help me process it, live it and share it. In Jesus' name I pray, amen.

What is God speaking to you? What action will you take in light of today's devotion?

#DontDoLifeAloneDevo #ReadPrayApplyRemain

1 Samuel 5:1-7:17, Psalms 106:13-31, Proverbs 14:32-33, John 6:1-21

May 10

"And they said, "Is not this Jesus, the son of
Joseph, whose father and mother we know?
How is it then that He says, 'I have come down
from heaven'?"" John 6:42

When you get close to something it can be easy
to take it for granted. The community where
Jesus grew up had a hard time accepting Him as
savior because of what they thought they knew
about Him. Don't miss what God has done and
is doing in your life. The best is yet to come.

Thank you God for another day and for your
word. Help me process it, live it and share it. In
Jesus' name I pray, amen.

What is God speaking to you? What action will
you take in light of today's devotion?

#DontDoLifeAloneDevo #ReadPrayApplyRemain

1 Samuel 8:1-9:27, Psalms 106:32-48, Proverbs
14:34-35, John 6:22-42

May 11

"For He satisfies the longing soul, and fills the hungry soul with goodness." Psalms 107:9

God wants to fill us up more than we want to be filled. Unfortunately, sometimes we turn to other sources to try and find the fulfillment that can only come from Him. If you are running on empty, turn to the well that will never run dry.

Thank you God for another day and for your word. Help me process it, live it and share it. In Jesus' name I pray, amen.

What is God speaking to you? What action will you take in light of today's devotion?

#DontDoLifeAloneDevo #ReadPrayApplyRemain

1 Samuel 10:1-11:15, Psalms 107:1-43, Proverbs 15:1-3, John 6:43-71

May 12

"A wholesome tongue is a tree of life, but perverseness in it breaks the spirit." Proverbs 15:4

What are you doing with your words? We have all been at the receiving end of words that break the spirit. Some people could care less about how they talk, but if our words have the ability to bring life, why not use them to do so?

Thank you God for another day and for your word. Help me process it, live it and share it. In Jesus' name I pray, amen.

What is God speaking to you? What action will you take in light of today's devotion?

#DontDoLifeAloneDevo #ReadPrayApplyRemain

1 Samuel 12:1-13:23, Psalms 108:1-13, Proverbs 15:4, John 7:1-30

May 13

"He who believes in Me, as the Scripture has said, out of his heart will flow rivers of living water." John 7:38

Incredible things come from having a relationship with Jesus. On top of hope and salvation, we have the opportunity to let all that God is doing overflow into the lives of people around us. Let the river flow and share the hope that you now have.

Thank you God for another day and for your word. Help me process it, live it and share it. In Jesus' name I pray, amen.

What is God speaking to you? What action will you take in light of today's devotion?

#DontDoLifeAloneDevo #ReadPrayApplyRemain

1 Samuel 14:1-52, Psalms 109:1-31, Proverbs 15:5-7, John 7:31-53

May 14

"But the LORD said to Samuel, "Do not look at his appearance or at his physical stature, because I have refused him. For the LORD does not see as man sees; for man looks at the outward appearance, but the LORD looks at the heart."" I Samuel 16:7

Nothing has changed since this passage of scripture was originally written. God still looks at our heart. How is yours doing today?

Thank you God for another day and for your word. Help me process it, live it and share it. In Jesus' name I pray, amen.

What is God speaking to you? What action will you take in light of today's devotion?

#DontDoLifeAloneDevo #ReadPrayApplyRemain

1 Samuel 15:1-16:23, Psalms 110:1-7, Proverbs 15:8-10, John 8:1-20

May 15

"David fastened his sword to his armor and tried to walk, for he had not tested them. And David said to Saul, "I cannot walk with these, for I have not tested them. " So David took them off." I Samuel 17:39

Saul tried to make David wear his armor. He was trying to help David, but David was not made to wear Saul's armor. Whether they are well meaning or not, you don't have to live to please people's expectations. Focus on what God has called you to do and do it His way.

Thank you God for another day and for your word. Help me process it, live it and share it. In Jesus' name I pray, amen.

What is God speaking to you? What action will you take in light of today's devotion?

#DontDoLifeAloneDevo #ReadPrayApplyRemain

1 Samuel 17:1-18:4, Psalms 111:1-10, Proverbs 15:11, John 8:21-30

May 16

"A merry heart makes a cheerful countenance, but by sorrow of the heart the spirit is broken." Proverbs 15:13

One of the benefits of having healthy relationships is the joy that comes with them. Sometimes you need to spend time with people that you can laugh with. Life on this side of eternity is too short to be miserable all of the time.

Thank you God for another day and for your word. Help me process it, live it and share it. In Jesus' name I pray, amen.

What is God speaking to you? What action will you take in light of today's devotion?

#DontDoLifeAloneDevo #ReadPrayApplyRemain

1 Samuel 18:5-19:24, Psalms 112:1-10, Proverbs 15:12-14, John 8:31-59

May 17

"He raises the poor out of the dust, and lifts the needy out of the ash heap." Psalms 113:7

No matter what life brings our way, we will never be in a position that is too far for God to reach out and move in our life. God can meet you at your point of need today. Let Him.

Thank you God for another day and for your word. Help me process it, live it and share it. In Jesus' name I pray, amen.

What is God speaking to you? What action will you take in light of today's devotion?

#DontDoLifeAloneDevo #ReadPrayApplyRemain

1 Samuel 20:1-21:15, Psalms 113:1-114:8, Proverbs 15:15-17, John 9:1-41

May 18

"The LORD has been mindful of us; He will bless us; He will bless the house of Israel; He will bless the house of Aaron." Psalms 115:12

This verse is just as true today as it was when it was written. God is more mindful of us than we realize. He is working in our life even if we don't see where or how. Keep on keeping on.

Thank you God for another day and for your word. Help me process it, live it and share it. In Jesus' name I pray, amen.

What is God speaking to you? What action will you take in light of today's devotion?

#DontDoLifeAloneDevo #ReadPrayApplyRemain

1 Samuel 22:1-23:29, Psalms 115:1-18, Proverbs 15:18-19, John 10:1-21

May 19

"I love the LORD, because He has heard my voice and my supplications." Psalms 116:1

Sometimes we focus on what we need God to do, but forget what He has already done. The Psalmist said, "He has heard my voice". God has already been so good to us. Let your love and life overflow from a place of gratitude first.

Thank you God for another day and for your word. Help me process it, live it and share it. In Jesus' name I pray, amen.

What is God speaking to you? What action will you take in light of today's devotion?

#DontDoLifeAloneDevo #ReadPrayApplyRemain

1 Samuel 24:1-25:44, Psalms 116:1-19, Proverbs 15:20-21, John 10:22-42

May 20

"A man has joy by the answer of his mouth, and a word spoken in due season, how good it is!" Proverbs 15:23

A few words can make a big impact when they are spoken at the right time. We have all benefited from timely words. Don't miss out on an opportunity to speak into some else's life today.

Thank you God for another day and for your word. Help me process it, live it and share it. In Jesus' name I pray, amen.

What is God speaking to you? What action will you take in light of today's devotion?

#DontDoLifeAloneDevo #ReadPrayApplyRemain

1 Samuel 26:1-28:25, Psalms 117:1-2, Proverbs 15:22-23, John 11:1-54

May 21

"It is better to trust in the LORD than to put confidence in princes." Psalms 118:9

God is the only one that will never let us down, but for whatever reason, we are prone to wonder. Some people and things talk a big game and over promise but under deliver. You do the trusting and let God do the fulfilling.

Thank you God for another day and for your word. Help me process it, live it and share it. In Jesus' name I pray, amen.

What is God speaking to you? What action will you take in light of today's devotion?

#DontDoLifeAloneDevo #ReadPrayApplyRemain

1 Samuel 29:1-31:13, Psalms 118:1-18, Proverbs 15:24-26, John 11:55-12:19

May 22

"I have come as a light into the world, that whoever believes in Me should not abide in darkness." John 12:46

Sometimes what we see as a problem God sees as an opportunity. Even in difficult seasons God wants us to be a light in the darkness. We need to walk in the light just as much as we need to share it.

Thank you God for another day and for your word. Help me process it, live it and share it. In Jesus' name I pray, amen.

What is God speaking to you? What action will you take in light of today's devotion?

#DontDoLifeAloneDevo #ReadPrayApplyRemain

2 Samuel 1:1-2:11, Psalms 118:19-29, Proverbs 15:27-28, John 12:20-50

May 23

"How can a young man cleanse his way? By taking heed according to Your word." Psalms 119:9

It's never too late to start over. Sometimes we get lost along the way. Thankfully, God gives us the grace to begin again and He offers us a road map in His word.

Thank you God for another day and for your word. Help me process it, live it and share it. In Jesus' name I pray, amen.

What is God speaking to you? What action will you take in light of today's devotion?

#DontDoLifeAloneDevo #ReadPrayApplyRemain

2 Samuel 2:12-3:39, Psalms 119:1-16, Proverbs 15:29-30, John 13:1-30

May 24

"So David said to Michal, "It was before the LORD, who chose me instead of your father and all his house, to appoint me ruler over the people of the LORD, over Israel. Therefore I will play music before the LORD."" II Samuel 6:21

David's wife was embarrassed when David started worshipping God because she felt that he got out of control. David did not hold back because he knew how faithful God had been to him. Don't let anyone or anything keep you from worshipping God with all of your heart.

Thank you God for another day and for your word. Help me process it, live it and share it. In Jesus' name I pray, amen.

What is God speaking to you? What action will you take in light of today's devotion?

#DontDoLifeAloneDevo #ReadPrayApplyRemain

2 Samuel 4:1-6:23, Psalms 119:17-32, Proverbs 15:31-32, John 13:31-14:14

May 25

"Turn away my eyes from looking at worthless things, and revive me in Your way." Psalms 119:37

Whatever you spend time focusing on is eventually the direction that you are going to head in. This prayer does not expose weakness as much as it reveals strength. Don't hesitate to take an inventory of where your focus is, make changes if needed, and then begin again.

Thank you God for another day and for your word. Help me process it, live it and share it. In Jesus' name I pray, amen.

What is God speaking to you? What action will you take in light of today's devotion?

#DontDoLifeAloneDevo #ReadPrayApplyRemain

2 Samuel 7:1-8:18, Psalms 119:33-48, Proverbs 15:33, John 14:15-31

May 26

"I am the vine; you are the branches. If you remain in me and I in you, you will bear much fruit; apart from me you can do nothing." John 15:5

The devotional that you are reading right now was written with this verse in mind. Regardless of your circumstances, if you are connected to the vine, nothing is impossible. Keep going and growing as you seek and trust God through prayer and time in His word.

Thank you God for another day and for your word. Help me process it, live it and share it. In Jesus' name I pray, amen.

What is God speaking to you? What action will you take in light of today's devotion?

#DontDoLifeAloneDevo #ReadPrayApplyRemain

2 Samuel 9:1-11:27, Psalms 119:49-64, Proverbs 16:1-3, John 15:1-27

May 27

"It is good for me that I have been afflicted, that I may learn Your statutes." Psalms 119:71

Nobody wants to face difficult circumstances but the truth is, God can use our struggles to help us grow. Our muscles do not grow without tearing first. God can redeem any situation. Don't allow your storms to be wasted. Learn and grow closer to Jesus in the good and the not so good seasons of life.

Thank you God for another day and for your word. Help me process it, live it and share it. In Jesus' name I pray, amen.

What is God speaking to you? What action will you take in light of today's devotion?

#DontDoLifeAloneDevo #ReadPrayApplyRemain

2 Samuel 12:1-31, Psalms 119:65-80, Proverbs 16:4-5, John 16:1-33

May 28

"When a man's ways please the LORD, He makes even his enemies to be at peace with him." Proverbs 16:7

Your relationship with God will overflow into every other area of your life eventually. If you are having a conflict with someone, focus more of your attention on Jesus then the situation. He can handle it better than you ever could.

Thank you God for another day and for your word. Help me process it, live it and share it. In Jesus' name I pray, amen.

What is God speaking to you? What action will you take in light of today's devotion?

#DontDoLifeAloneDevo #ReadPrayApplyRemain

2 Samuel 13:1-39, Psalms 119:81-96, Proverbs 16:6-7, John 17:1-26

May 29

"Your word is a lamp to my feet and a light to my path." Psalms 119:105

When this verse was written they did not have headlights or LED flashlights. In order for a candle or at most an oil lamp to light the path, the person holding the light had to continue walking by faith. Every step revealed more of the path. This truth is still applicable.

Thank you God for another day and for your word. Help me process it, live it and share it. In Jesus' name I pray, amen.

What is God speaking to you? What action will you take in light of today's devotion?

#DontDoLifeAloneDevo #ReadPrayApplyRemain

2 Samuel 14:1-15:22, Psalms 119:97-112, Proverbs 16:8-9, John 18:1-24

May 30

"Now the king and all the people who were with him became weary; so they refreshed themselves there." 2 Samuel 16:14

Sometimes we grow weary. Our culture tells us to keep on pushing regardless of the fall out, but sometimes you need to take some time to recharge. In order to keep going tomorrow you may need to rest today.

Thank you God for another day and for your word. Help me process it, live it and share it. In Jesus' name I pray, amen.

What is God speaking to you? What action will you take in light of today's devotion?

#DontDoLifeAloneDevo #ReadPrayApplyRemain

2 Samuel 15:23-16:23, Psalms 119:113-128, Proverbs 16:10-11, John 18:25-19:22

May 31

"Your testimonies are wonderful; Therefore my soul keeps them." Psalms 119:129

Remembering what God has already done will help keep you going when things get difficult. Keep the testimonies alive.

Thank you God for another day and for your word. Help me process it, live it and share it. In Jesus' name I pray, amen.

What is God speaking to you? What action will you take in light of today's devotion?

#DontDoLifeAloneDevo #ReadPrayApplyRemain

2 Samuel 17:1-29, Psalms 119:129-152, Proverbs 16:12-13, John 19:23-19:42

June 1

"Jesus said to him, "Thomas, because you have seen Me, you have believed. Blessed are those who have not seen and yet have believed.""
John 20:29

There are times that we hesitate to make a move before we see God move. What if God is waiting for us to take our next step by faith before He moves?

Thank you God for another day and for your word. Help me process it, live it and share it. In Jesus' name I pray, amen.

What is God speaking to you? What action will you take in light of today's devotion?

#DontDoLifeAloneDevo #ReadPrayApplyRemain

2 Samuel 18:1-19:10, Psalms 119:153-176, Proverbs 16:14-15, John 20:1-31

June 2

"And He said to them, "Cast the net on the right side of the boat, and you will find some." So they cast, and now they were not able to draw it in because of the multitude of fish." John 21:6

These skilled fishermen were having a bad day until Jesus showed up. After they followed His instructions their haul went from nothing to too much. Provision follows obedience and trust. God is good at what He does.

Thank you God for another day and for your word. Help me process it, live it and share it. In Jesus' name I pray, amen.

What is God speaking to you? What action will you take in light of today's devotion?

#DontDoLifeAloneDevo #ReadPrayApplyRemain

2 Samuel 19:11-20:13, Psalms 120:1-7, Proverbs 16:16-17, John 21:1-25

June 3

"But you shall receive power when the Holy Spirit has come upon you; and you shall be witnesses to Me in Jerusalem, and in all Judea and Samaria, and to the end of the earth."" Acts 1:8

Most of our failures can be attributed to us walking alone. If you want to overcome an obstacle or make a difference with your life, seek the Lord. Holy Spirt will do more in and through you than you could ever accomplish on your own.

Thank you God for another day and for your word. Help me process it, live it and share it. In Jesus' name I pray, amen.

What is God speaking to you? What action will you take in light of today's devotion?

#DontDoLifeAloneDevo #ReadPrayApplyRemain

2 Samuel 20:14-21:22, Psalms 121:1-8, Proverbs 16:18, Acts 1:1-26

June 4

"Praising God and having favor with all the people. And the Lord added to the church daily those who were being saved." Acts 2:47

When the Holy Spirit shows up and people are doing life together, life change takes place. This verse says, daily people were being saved. That's worth living for.

Thank you God for another day and for your word. Help me process it, live it and share it. In Jesus' name I pray, amen.

What is God speaking to you? What action will you take in light of today's devotion?

#DontDoLifeAloneDevo #ReadPrayApplyRemain

2 Samuel 22:1-23:23, Psalms 122:1-9, Proverbs 16:19-20, Acts 2:1-47

June 5

"Then Peter said, "Silver and gold I do not have, but what I do have I give you: In the name of Jesus Christ of Nazareth, rise up and walk.""
Acts 3:6

You don't have to have a ton of resources to make an impact. If you have Jesus, He will provide. Point people to the Lord and let Him handle the details.

Thank you God for another day and for your word. Help me process it, live it and share it. In Jesus' name I pray, amen.

What is God speaking to you? What action will you take in light of today's devotion?

#DontDoLifeAloneDevo #ReadPrayApplyRemain

2 Samuel 23:24-24:25, Psalms 123:1-4, Proverbs 16:21-23, Acts 3:1-26

June 6

"Now when they saw the boldness of Peter and John, and perceived that they were uneducated and untrained men, they marveled. And they realized that they had been with Jesus." Acts 4:13

If people know you as a person that spends time with Jesus, you are heading in the right direction. He still uses the foolish things of the world to confound the wise.

Thank you God for another day and for your word. Help me process it, live it and share it. In Jesus' name I pray, amen.

What is God speaking to you? What action will you take in light of today's devotion?

#DontDoLifeAloneDevo #ReadPrayApplyRemain

1 Kings 1:1-53, Psalms 124:1-8, Proverbs 16:24, Acts 4:1-37

June 7

"But if it is of God, you cannot overthrow it—lest you even be found to fight against God."" Acts 5:39

God's plan will prevail. Move forward in courage and be encouraged because the Lord is with you.

Thank you God for another day and for your word. Help me process it, live it and share it. In Jesus' name I pray, amen.

What is God speaking to you? What action will you take in light of today's devotion?

#DontDoLifeAloneDevo #ReadPrayApplyRemain

1 Kings 2:1-3:2, Psalms 125:1-5, Proverbs 16:25, Acts 5:1-42

June 8

"And God gave Solomon wisdom and exceedingly great understanding, and largeness of heart like the sand on the seashore." I Kings 4:29

Solomon did not always get it right but when He asked God to move in his life, wisdom was at the top of his list. Not a bad place to start.

Thank you God for another day and for your word. Help me process it, live it and share it. In Jesus' name I pray, amen.

What is God speaking to you? What action will you take in light of today's devotion?

#DontDoLifeAloneDevo #ReadPrayApplyRemain

1 Kings 3:3-4:34, Psalms 126:1-6, Proverbs 16:26-27, Acts 6:1-15

June 9

"Unless the LORD builds the house, They labor in vain who build it; Unless the LORD guards the city, The watchman stays awake in vain." Psalms 127:1

You can do a lot of good stuff and still miss some God stuff. Playing the background is not a bad position to be in. Let God take the lead. He is better at what He does than we could ever be.

Thank you God for another day and for your word. Help me process it, live it and share it. In Jesus' name I pray, amen.

What is God speaking to you? What action will you take in light of today's devotion?

#DontDoLifeAloneDevo #ReadPrayApplyRemain

1 Kings 5:1-6:38, Psalms 127:1-5, Proverbs 16:28-30, Acts 7:1-29

June 10

"However, the Most High does not dwell in temples made with hands, as the prophet says." Acts 7:48

After Jesus died and rose again, the early church was birthed. Our faith is not just about where we go on Sunday morning, but who we are becoming. We are the temple of the Holy Spirit. How can God be most glorified in your life today?

Thank you God for another day and for your word. Help me process it, live it and share it. In Jesus' name I pray, amen.

What is God speaking to you? What action will you take in light of today's devotion?

#DontDoLifeAloneDevo #ReadPrayApplyRemain

1 Kings 7:1-51, Psalms 128:1-6, Proverbs 16:31-33, Acts 7:30-50

June 11

"Then he knelt down and cried out with a loud voice, "Lord, do not charge them with this sin." And when he had said this, he fell asleep." Acts 7:60

While Stephen was being stoned to death because of his faith, he was praying for the people that were in the process of ending his life. They could not take his life because He already gave that to Christ. Stephen's life and death are a great example of what it looks like to trust the Lord.

Thank you God for another day and for your word. Help me process it, live it and share it. In Jesus' name I pray, amen.

What is God speaking to you? What action will you take in light of today's devotion?

#DontDoLifeAloneDevo #ReadPrayApplyRemain

1 Kings 8:1-66, Psalms 129:1-8, Proverbs 17:1, Acts 7:51-8:13

June 12

"The refining pot is for silver and the furnace for gold, but the LORD tests the hearts." Proverbs 17:3

Heaven and eternity with the Lord are a part of God's plan but so is the journey. Sometimes the process is the point. Don't miss the value in the moments.

Thank you God for another day and for your word. Help me process it, live it and share it. In Jesus' name I pray, amen.

What is God speaking to you? What action will you take in light of today's devotion?

#DontDoLifeAloneDevo #ReadPrayApplyRemain

1 Kings 9:1-10:29, Psalms 130:1-8, Proverbs 17:2-3, Acts 8:14-40

June 13

"Then all who heard were amazed, and said, "Is this not he who destroyed those who called on this name in Jerusalem, and has come here for that purpose, so that he might bring them bound to the chief priests?"" Acts 9:21

Paul's life changed so much that people did not know what to do with him. Your actions will testify to the change taking place in your life. Be patient and let God finish His work.

Thank you God for another day and for your word. Help me process it, live it and share it. In Jesus' name I pray, amen.

What is God speaking to you? What action will you take in light of today's devotion?

#DontDoLifeAloneDevo #ReadPrayApplyRemain

1 Kings 11:1-12:19, Psalms 131:1-3, Proverbs 17:4-5, Acts 9:1-25

June 14

"But Barnabas took him and brought him to the apostles. And he declared to them how he had seen the Lord on the road, and that He had spoken to him, and how he had preached boldly at Damascus in the name of Jesus." Acts 9:27

God can use you to speak up for and speak into other people. Our life is not just about us. Barnabas was a great encourager. May the same be said about us.

Thank you God for another day and for your word. Help me process it, live it and share it. In Jesus' name I pray, amen.

What is God speaking to you? What action will you take in light of today's devotion?

#DontDoLifeAloneDevo #ReadPrayApplyRemain

1 Kings 12:20-13:34, Psalms 132:1-18, Proverbs 17:6, Acts 9:26-43

June 15

"Behold, how good and how pleasant it is for brethren to dwell together in unity!" Psalm 133:1

Our differences can look like a weakness in our relationships, but they are actually a strength. Every part of our body has a different function, but every part matters. We don't have to be the same to accomplish great things together.

Thank you God for another day and for your word. Help me process it, live it and share it. In Jesus' name I pray, amen.

What is God speaking to you? What action will you take in light of today's devotion?

#DontDoLifeAloneDevo #ReadPrayApplyRemain

1 Kings 14:1-15:24, Psalms 133:1-3, Proverbs 17:7-8, Acts 10:1-23

June 16

"He who covers a transgression seeks love, but he who repeats a matter separates friends."
Proverbs 17:9

God's word reminds us that love keeps no record of wrongs. Keep the past in the past. Walk in forgiveness and be free in Jesus name.

Thank you God for another day and for your word. Help me process it, live it and share it. In Jesus' name I pray, amen.

What is God speaking to you? What action will you take in light of today's devotion?

#DontDoLifeAloneDevo #ReadPrayApplyRemain

1 Kings 15:25-17:24, Psalms 134:1-3, Proverbs 17:9-11, Acts 10:24-48

June 17

"Whoever rewards evil for good, evil will not depart from his house." Proverbs 17:13

Just because something is popular, it does not make it right. Focus on living in a way that pleases the Lord, and let God handle the rest. We reap what we sow. It's never a bad time to do what's right.

Thank you God for another day and for your word. Help me process it, live it and share it. In Jesus' name I pray, amen.

What is God speaking to you? What action will you take in light of today's devotion?

#DontDoLifeAloneDevo #ReadPrayApplyRemain

1 Kings 18:1-46, Psalms 135:1-21, Proverbs 17:12-13, Acts 11:1-30

June 18

"And after the earthquake a fire, but the LORD was not in the fire; and after the fire a still small voice." I Kings 19:12

God spoke to Moses through a burning bush, but He only did that once. Don't be surprised if God speaks to you today in an unconventional way.

Thank you God for another day and for your word. Help me process it, live it and share it. In Jesus' name I pray, amen.

What is God speaking to you? What action will you take in light of today's devotion?

#DontDoLifeAloneDevo #ReadPrayApplyRemain

1 Kings 19:1-21, Psalms 136:1-26, Proverbs 17:14-15, Acts 12:1-23

June 19

"But the word of God grew and multiplied."
Acts 12:24

In the New Testament we see that God grew the church during difficult seasons. Just because things are tough, it doesn't mean that God has forgotten about you. In fact, it may mean that God is doing a great work in your life.

Thank you God for another day and for your word. Help me process it, live it and share it. In Jesus' name I pray, amen.

What is God speaking to you? What action will you take in light of today's devotion?

#DontDoLifeAloneDevo #ReadPrayApplyRemain

1 Kings 20:1-21:29, Psalms 137:1-9, Proverbs 17:16, Acts 12:24-13:15

June 20

"A friend loves at all times, and a brother is born for adversity." Proverbs 17:17

It's great to have friends to celebrate with, but our relationships gain their greatest value when things are difficult. Build your relationships on commitment, not just convenience. Don't do life alone.

Thank you God for another day and for your word. Help me process it, live it and share it. In Jesus' name I pray, amen.

What is God speaking to you? What action will you take in light of today's devotion?

#DontDoLifeAloneDevo #ReadPrayApplyRemain

1 Kings 22:1-53, Psalms 138:1-8, Proverbs 17:17-18, Acts 13:16-13:41

June 21

"And the disciples were filled with joy and with the Holy Spirit." Acts 13:52

There is so much competing for space in our life. Let God fill you up first. He will make everything else better and satisfy like nothing else can.

Thank you God for another day and for your word. Help me process it, live it and share it. In Jesus' name I pray, amen.

What is God speaking to you? What action will you take in light of today's devotion?

#DontDoLifeAloneDevo #ReadPrayApplyRemain

2 Kings 1:1-2:25, Psalms 139:1-24, Proverbs 17:19-21, Acts 13:42-14:7

June 22

"And he said, "Thus says the LORD: 'Make this valley full of ditches.'" II Kings 3:16

We all want God to move but are we positioned to receive all that He has for us? You may find yourself in a drought, but God may be waiting for you to dig some ditches for Him to fill up. Walking by faith is not always easy, but it will always be worth it.

Thank you God for another day and for your word. Help me process it, live it and share it. In Jesus' name I pray, amen.

What is God speaking to you? What action will you take in light of today's devotion?

#DontDoLifeAloneDevo #ReadPrayApplyRemain

2 Kings 3:1-4:17, Psalms 140:1-13, Proverbs 17:22, Acts 14:8-28

June 23

"Therefore I judge that we should not trouble those from among the Gentiles who are turning to God." Acts 15:19

God is trying to reach His lost sons and daughters and He has issued us an invitation to be a part of the rescue team. We need to stop being a barrier and start building bridges.

Thank you God for another day and for your word. Help me process it, live it and share it. In Jesus' name I pray, amen.

What is God speaking to you? What action will you take in light of today's devotion?

#DontDoLifeAloneDevo #ReadPrayApplyRemain

2 Kings 4:18-5:27, Psalms 141:1-10, Proverbs 17:23, Acts 15:1-35

June 24

"So the man of God said, "Where did it fall?" And he showed him the place. So he cut off a stick, and threw it in there; and he made the iron float." 2 Kings 6:6

Sometimes our situations look impossible, but God may not be done working in this particular chapter in your story. When our faith intersects with God's power, the plot changes.

Thank you God for another day and for your word. Help me process it, live it and share it. In Jesus' name I pray, amen.

What is God speaking to you? What action will you take in light of today's devotion?

#DontDoLifeAloneDevo #ReadPrayApplyRemain

2 Kings 6:1-7:20, Psalms 142:1-7, Proverbs 17:24-25, Acts 15:36-16:15

June 25

"But at midnight Paul and Silas were praying and singing hymns to God, and the prisoners were listening to them." Acts 16:25

Paul and Silas did not worship God because their circumstances were good. They chose that response because God is good even when you find yourself wrongfully in prison. Don't stop praising God regardless of what season you find yourself in.

Thank you God for another day and for your word. Help me process it, live it and share it. In Jesus' name I pray, amen.

What is God speaking to you? What action will you take in light of today's devotion?

#DontDoLifeAloneDevo #ReadPrayApplyRemain

2 Kings 8:1-9:13, Psalms 143:1-12, Proverbs 17:26, Acts 16:16-40

June 26

"Therefore he reasoned in the synagogue with the Jews and with the Gentile worshipers, and in the marketplace daily with those who happened to be there." Acts 17:17

Wherever we find ourselves, we have an opportunity to share Jesus. People are looking for hope. Tell them.

Thank you God for another day and for your word. Help me process it, live it and share it. In Jesus' name I pray, amen.

What is God speaking to you? What action will you take in light of today's devotion?

#DontDoLifeAloneDevo #ReadPrayApplyRemain

2 Kings 9:14-10:31, Psalms 144:1-15, Proverbs 17:27-28, Acts 17:1-34

June 27

"Every day I will bless You, and I will praise Your name forever and ever." Psalms 145:2

You have a lot to do today. God does too, but He still gave you another day. Don't forget to say thank you.

Thank you God for another day and for your word. Help me process it, live it and share it. In Jesus' name I pray, amen.

What is God speaking to you? What action will you take in light of today's devotion?

#DontDoLifeAloneDevo #ReadPrayApplyRemain

2 Kings 10:32-12:21, Psalms 145:1-21, Proverbs 18:1, Acts 18:1-22

June 28

"So that even handkerchiefs or aprons were brought from his body to the sick, and the diseases left them and the evil spirits went out of them." Acts 19:12

God can move however He wants to. Don't limit your expectations and you will see Him show up and show out.

Thank you God for another day and for your word. Help me process it, live it and share it. In Jesus' name I pray, amen.

What is God speaking to you? What action will you take in light of today's devotion?

#DontDoLifeAloneDevo #ReadPrayApplyRemain

2 Kings 13:1-14:29, Psalms 146:1-10, Proverbs 18:2-3, Acts 18:23-19:12

June 29

"He counts the number of the stars; He calls them all by name."
Psalms 147:4

The God that created the world, made you. He knows every star and He has the hairs on your head or lack there of, numbered. God is more mindful of you than you realize.

Thank you God for another day and for your word. Help me process it, live it and share it. In Jesus' name I pray, amen.

What is God speaking to you? What action will you take in light of today's devotion?

#DontDoLifeAloneDevo #ReadPrayApplyRemain

2 Kings 15:1-16:20, Psalms 147:1-20, Proverbs 18:4-5, Acts 19:13-41

June 30

"But none of these things move me; nor do I count my life dear to myself, so that I may finish my race with joy, and the ministry which I received from the Lord Jesus, to testify to the gospel of the grace of God." Acts 20:24

Our life is about so much more than just us. It's great to start off well, but even better to finish well. A rich life has nothing to do with money.

Thank you God for another day and for your word. Help me process it, live it and share it. In Jesus' name I pray, amen.

What is God speaking to you? What action will you take in light of today's devotion?

#DontDoLifeAloneDevo #ReadPrayApplyRemain

2 Kings 17:1-18:12, Psalms 148:1-14, Proverbs 18:6-7, Acts 20:1-38

July 1

"For the LORD delights in his people; he crowns the humble with victory." Psalms 149:4

When we face opposition, our flesh wants to puff up in defense. According to this verse, humility wins the battle. Choose to walk in humility and watch and see how God works in your life.

Thank you God for another day and for your word. Help me process it, live it and share it. In Jesus' name I pray, amen.

What is God speaking to you? What action will you take in light of today's devotion?

#DontDoLifeAloneDevo #ReadPrayApplyRemain

2 Kings 18:13-19:37, Psalms 149:1-9, Proverbs 18:8, Acts 21:1-17

July 2

"He who is slothful in his work is a brother to him who is a great destroyer." Proverbs 18:9

Being lazy can cost us more than productivity. Pray hard, work hard and play hard. You won't regret it.

Thank you God for another day and for your word. Help me process it, live it and share it. In Jesus' name I pray, amen.

What is God speaking to you? What action will you take in light of today's devotion?

#DontDoLifeAloneDevo #ReadPrayApplyRemain

2 Kings 20:1-22:2, Psalms 150:1-6, Proverbs 18:9-10, Acts 21:18-36

July 3

"Then he said, 'The God of our fathers has chosen you that you should know His will, and see the Just One, and hear the voice of His mouth." Acts 22:14

God wants to make Himself known to you. Seek Him and you will find Him.

Thank you God for another day and for your word. Help me process it, live it and share it. In Jesus' name I pray, amen.

What is God speaking to you? What action will you take in light of today's devotion?

#DontDoLifeAloneDevo #ReadPrayApplyRemain

2 Kings 22:3-23:30, Psalms 1:1-6, Proverbs 18:11-12, Acts 21:37-22:16

July 4

"He who answers a matter before he hears it, it is folly and shame to him." Proverbs 18:13

We have two ears and one mouth for a reason. If you want to grow, you have to take time listen. You may have something to say, but if you don't listen, you won't have anything to say that's worth listening to.

Thank you God for another day and for your word. Help me process it, live it and share it. In Jesus' name I pray, amen.

What is God speaking to you? What action will you take in light of today's devotion?

#DontDoLifeAloneDevo #ReadPrayApplyRemain

2 Kings 23:31-25:30, Psalms 2:1-12, Proverbs 18:13, Acts 22:17-23:10

July 5

"I lay down and slept; I awoke, for the LORD sustained me." Psalms 3:5

God is working on our behalf around the clock. On more than one occasion God has done something in our life that sustained us through a circumstance, and we were not even aware of the need because He took care of it. We can trust him.

Thank you God for another day and for your word. Help me process it, live it and share it. In Jesus' name I pray, amen.

What is God speaking to you? What action will you take in light of today's devotion?

#DontDoLifeAloneDevo #ReadPrayApplyRemain

1 Chronicles 1:1-2:17, Psalms 3:1-8, Proverbs 18:14-15, Acts 23:11-35

July 6

"A man's gift makes room for him, and brings him before great men." Proverbs 18:16

God gave us talents and abilities for a reason. Don't waste them. We never know what God may have in store. Let Him take the lead.

Thank you God for another day and for your word. Help me process it, live it and share it. In Jesus' name I pray, amen.

What is God speaking to you? What action will you take in light of today's devotion?

#DontDoLifeAloneDevo #ReadPrayApplyRemain

1 Chronicles 2:18-4:4, Psalms 4:1-8, Proverbs 18:16-18, Acts 24:1-27

July 7

"And Jabez called on the God of Israel saying, "Oh, that You would bless me indeed, and enlarge my territory, that Your hand would be with me, and that You would keep me from evil, that I may not cause pain!" So God granted him what he requested." I Chronicles 4:10

Jabez was not afraid to ask God to move in his life. Don't miss out on an opportunity to trust God for big things. Walking by faith changes everything.

Thank you God for another day and for your word. Help me process it, live it and share it. In Jesus' name I pray, amen.

What is God speaking to you? What action will you take in light of today's devotion?

#DontDoLifeAloneDevo #ReadPrayApplyRemain

1 Chronicles 4:5-5:17, Psalms 5:1-12, Proverbs 18:19, Acts 25:1-27

July 8

"Death and life are in the power of the tongue, and those who love it will eat its fruit." Proverbs 18:21

Our words are powerful. They have the power to build up or tear down. Words have the ability to change the trajectory of someone's day, or maybe even their life. Speak life!

Thank you God for another day and for your word. Help me process it, live it and share it. In Jesus' name I pray, amen.

What is God speaking to you? What action will you take in light of today's devotion?

#DontDoLifeAloneDevo #ReadPrayApplyRemain

1 Chronicles 5:18-6:81, Psalms 6:1-10, Proverbs 18:20-21, Acts 26:1-32

July 9

"Oh, let the wickedness of the wicked come to an end, but establish the just; for the righteous God tests the hearts and minds." Psalms 7:9

We cannot always control our circumstances, but we can control our response. Prayer changes things, but it also changes us. If you are living in a way that is unpleasing to the Lord, He can help you correct your course. Let Him.

Thank you God for another day and for your word. Help me process it, live it and share it. In Jesus' name I pray, amen.

What is God speaking to you? What action will you take in light of today's devotion?

#DontDoLifeAloneDevo #ReadPrayApplyRemain

1 Chronicles 7:1-8:40, Psalms 7:1-17, Proverbs 18:22, Acts 27:1-20

July 10

"A man who has friends must himself be friendly, but there is a friend who sticks closer than a brother." Proverbs 18:24

Some friends are a part of our life for a short season, but some are for the long haul. Regardless, Jesus remains. When things fall apart and others walk away, Jesus is still there.

Thank you God for another day and for your word. Help me process it, live it and share it. In Jesus' name I pray, amen.

What is God speaking to you? What action will you take in light of today's devotion?

#DontDoLifeAloneDevo #ReadPrayApplyRemain

1 Chronicles 9:1-10:14, Psalms 8:1-9, Proverbs 18:23-24, Acts 27:21-44

July 11

"I will praise You, O Lord, with my whole heart; I will tell of all Your marvelous works." Psalms 9:1

Usually when you see a good movie, read a good story or enjoy a good meal, you tell somebody. Because of the love, grace and goodness of God, I am far better off than I deserve. Our world desperately needs hope. Reflect on where you found hope, and don't forget to tell somebody.

Thank you God for another day and for your word. Help me process it, live it and share it. In Jesus' name I pray, amen.

What is God speaking to you? What action will you take in light of today's devotion?

#DontDoLifeAloneDevo #ReadPrayApplyRemain

1 Chronicles 11:1-12:18, Psalms 9:1-12, Proverbs 19:1-3, Acts 28:1-31

July 12

"For I am not ashamed of the gospel of Christ, for it is the power of God to salvation for everyone who believes, for the Jew first and also for the Greek."
Romans 1:16

Some people look at faith as a crutch, but for me it's full on life support. Putting my trust in Jesus and choosing to follow Him changed everything for me. The hope we find in Jesus is good news and that's worth talking about.

Thank you God for another day and for your word. Help me process it, live it and share it. In Jesus' name I pray, amen.

What is God speaking to you? What action will you take in light of today's devotion?

#DontDoLifeAloneDevo #ReadPrayApplyRemain

1 Chronicles 12:19-14:17, Psalms 9:13-20, Proverbs 19:4-5, Romans 1:1-17

July 13

"And it happened, as the ark of the covenant of the Lord came to the City of David, that Michal, Saul's daughter, looked through a window and saw King David whirling and playing music; and she despised him in her heart." I Chronicles 15:29

Do not let the things that are going wrong hinder you from worshiping God. The opinion of others has nothing to do with the goodness of God in your life.

Thank you God for another day and for your word. Help me process it, live it and share it. In Jesus' name I pray, amen.

What is God speaking to you? What action will you take in light of today's devotion?

#DontDoLifeAloneDevo #ReadPrayApplyRemain

1 Chronicles 15:1-16:36, Psalms 10:1-15, Proverbs 19:6-7, Romans 1:18-32

July 14

"He who gets wisdom loves his own soul; He who keeps understanding will find good."
Proverbs 19:8

Wisdom and understanding will lead to so many great things. Seek the Lord and let Him lead you.

Thank you God for another day and for your word. Help me process it, live it and share it. In Jesus' name I pray, amen.

What is God speaking to you? What action will you take in light of today's devotion?

#DontDoLifeAloneDevo #ReadPrayApplyRemain

1 Chronicles 16:37-18:17, Psalms 10:16-18, Proverbs 19:8-9, Romans 2:1-24

July 15

"For what if some did not believe? Will their unbelief make the faithfulness of God without effect?" Romans 3:3

Change is inevitable, but there is one thing that we can count on regardless of what else is happening around us. God is faithful.

Thank you God for another day and for your word. Help me process it, live it and share it. In Jesus' name I pray, amen.

What is God speaking to you? What action will you take in light of today's devotion?

#DontDoLifeAloneDevo #ReadPrayApplyRemain

1 Chronicles 19:1-21:30, Psalms 11:1-7, Proverbs 19:10-12, Romans 2:25-3:8

July 16

"To stand every morning to thank and praise the Lord, and likewise at evening;" I Chronicles 23:30

There were specific instructions given for those that built and served in the temple. Praising God every day should continue on.

Thank you God for another day and for your word. Help me process it, live it and share it. In Jesus' name I pray, amen.

What is God speaking to you? What action will you take in light of today's devotion?

#DontDoLifeAloneDevo #ReadPrayApplyRemain

1 Chronicles 22:1-23:32, Psalms 12:1-8, Proverbs 19:13-14, Romans 3:9-31

July 17

"But I have trusted in Your mercy; My heart shall rejoice in Your salvation." Psalms 13:5

In the verses prior to this, David's concerns sound familiar when he is asking where God is and when He is going to move in his situation. Then he closes out by acknowledging God's mercy and salvation. Walking by faith is not always easy, but it will always be worth it.

Thank you God for another day and for your word. Help me process it, live it and share it. In Jesus' name I pray, amen.

What is God speaking to you? What action will you take in light of today's devotion?

#DontDoLifeAloneDevo #ReadPrayApplyRemain

1 Chronicles 24:1-26:11, Psalms 13:1-6, Proverbs 19:15-16, Romans 4:1-12

July 18

"Now hope does not disappoint, because the love of God has been poured out in our hearts by the Holy Spirit who was given to us." Romans 5:5

There are a lot of things in the world that over promise but under deliver. Jesus is not one of those things. He offers us a hope that does not disappoint. Trust Him.

Thank you God for another day and for your word. Help me process it, live it and share it. In Jesus' name I pray, amen.

What is God speaking to you? What action will you take in light of today's devotion?

#DontDoLifeAloneDevo #ReadPrayApplyRemain

1 Chronicles 26:12-27:34, Psalms 14:1-7, Proverbs 19:17, Romans 4:13-5:5

July 19

"But God demonstrates His own love toward us, in that while we were still sinners, Christ died for us." Romans 5:8

We don't have to get ourselves together before we turn to God. Jesus loves us. Jesus loves you. Jesus loves me. The cross and empty grave are more than enough and tell that part of the story so well.

Thank you God for another day and for your word. Help me process it, live it and share it. In Jesus' name I pray, amen.

What is God speaking to you? What action will you take in light of today's devotion?

#DontDoLifeAloneDevo #ReadPrayApplyRemain

1 Chronicles 28:1-29:30, Psalms 15:1-5, Proverbs 19:18-19, Romans 5:6-21

July 20

"You will show me the path of life; In Your presence is fullness of joy; At Your right hand are pleasures forevermore." Psalms 16:11

Faith is not just about the things we do, but the experiences that come from a God that loves us. The life and joy that God offers to us can't be found anywhere else. Enjoy the journey.

Thank you God for another day and for your word. Help me process it, live it and share it. In Jesus' name I pray, amen.

What is God speaking to you? What action will you take in light of today's devotion?

#DontDoLifeAloneDevo #ReadPrayApplyRemain

2 Chronicles 1:1-3:17, Psalms 16:1-11, Proverbs 19:20-21, Romans 6:1-23

July 21

"The fear of the Lord leads to life, and he who has it will abide in satisfaction; He will not be visited with evil." Proverbs 19:23

Some of the bible can be tough to process in the english language and this verse is one that we can wrestle with. The thought of the fear of the Lord is not intended to threaten or manipulate us into submission as it at times has been communicated. But to understand that an all powerful God that created the world loves us and is always working to reconcile us unto Him. That's incredible!

Thank you God for another day and for your word. Help me process it, live it and share it. In Jesus' name I pray, amen.

What is God speaking to you? What action will you take in light of today's devotion?

#DontDoLifeAloneDevo #ReadPrayApplyRemain

2 Chronicles 4:1-6:11, Psalms 17:1-15, Proverbs 19:22-23, Romans 7:1-13

July 22

"There is therefore now no condemnation to those who are in Christ Jesus, who do not walk according to the flesh, but according to the Spirit." Romans 8:1

Regret, shame and the fear of failing again want to hold us back from moving forward in our life. The forgiveness and grace of God do the exact opposite.

Thank you God for another day and for your word. Help me process it, live it and share it. In Jesus' name I pray, amen.

What is God speaking to you? What action will you take in light of today's devotion?

#DontDoLifeAloneDevo #ReadPrayApplyRemain

2 Chronicles 6:12-8:10, Psalms 18:1-15, Proverbs 19:24-25, Romans 7:14-8:8

July 23

"For I consider that the sufferings of this present time are not worthy to be compared with the glory which shall be revealed in us." Romans 8:18

Regardless of what life looks like on this side of eternity, there are even greater things that are yet to come. God is not finished with your story.

Thank you God for another day and for your word. Help me process it, live it and share it. In Jesus' name I pray, amen.

What is God speaking to you? What action will you take in light of today's devotion?

#DontDoLifeAloneDevo #ReadPrayApplyRemain

2 Chronicles 8:11-10:19, Psalms 18:16-36, Proverbs 19:26, Romans 8:9-25

July 24

"What then shall we say to these things? If God is for us, who can be against us?" Romans 8:31

Regardless of what you may be facing, when God is for you, that is more than enough. Everything changes when you operate from a place of victory knowing that God is in your corner.

Thank you God for another day and for your word. Help me process it, live it and share it. In Jesus' name I pray, amen.

What is God speaking to you? What action will you take in light of today's devotion?

#DontDoLifeAloneDevo #ReadPrayApplyRemain

2 Chronicles 11:1-13:22, Psalms 18:37-50, Proverbs 19:27-29, Romans 8:26-39

July 25

"The heavens declare the glory of God; the skies proclaim the work of his hands." Psalms 19:1

We can't see the wind, but we see the effects of the wind. We may not be able to see God as we see each other, but His handiwork is all around us. If you want to see and appreciate some of His work, glance up at his ever-changing canvas that we call the sky.

Thank you God for another day and for your word. Help me process it, live it and share it. In Jesus' name I pray, amen.

What is God speaking to you? What action will you take in light of today's devotion?

#DontDoLifeAloneDevo #ReadPrayApplyRemain

2 Chronicles 14:1-16:14, Psalms 19:1-14, Proverbs 20:1, Romans 9:1-24

July 26

"Some trust in chariots and some in horses, but we trust in the name of the Lord our God."
Psalms 20:7

We put our trust in things and people all the time that will eventually let us down. God is faithful and trustworthy.

Thank you God for another day and for your word. Help me process it, live it and share it. In Jesus' name I pray, amen.

What is God speaking to you? What action will you take in light of today's devotion?

#DontDoLifeAloneDevo #ReadPrayApplyRemain

2 Chronicles 17:1-18:34, Psalms 20:1-9, Proverbs 20:2-3, Romans 9:25-10:13

July 27

"How then shall they call on Him in whom they have not believed? And how shall they believe in Him of whom they have not heard? And how shall they hear without a preacher?" Romans 10:14

The world is looking for hope. We tell people about a good book we read or movie we watched. We tell people about a good meal we had. Tell them about the one that changes everything. Tell them about Jesus.

Thank you God for another day and for your word. Help me process it, live it and share it. In Jesus' name I pray, amen.

What is God speaking to you? What action will you take in light of today's devotion?

#DontDoLifeAloneDevo #ReadPrayApplyRemain

2 Chronicles 19:1-20:37, Psalms 21:1-13, Proverbs 20:4-6, Romans 10:14-11:12

July 28

"For the gifts and the calling of God are irrevocable." Romans 11:29

God has not changed his mind about the gifts that He put inside of you or the things that He wants to do in and through your life. You were created for more. Don't settle for less.

Thank you God for another day and for your word. Help me process it, live it and share it. In Jesus' name I pray, amen.

What is God speaking to you? What action will you take in light of today's devotion?

#DontDoLifeAloneDevo #ReadPrayApplyRemain

2 Chronicles 21:1-23:21, Psalms 22:1-18, Proverbs 20:7, Romans 11:13-36

July 29

"Having then gifts differing according to the grace that is given to us, let us use them: if prophecy, let us prophesy in proportion to our faith;"
Romans 12:6

The world needs what you bring to the table. The body of Christ needs what you bring to the table. You were uniquely designed by God to do incredible things. Never discount your significance.

Thank you God for another day and for your word. Help me process it, live it and share it. In Jesus' name I pray, amen.

What is God speaking to you? What action will you take in light of today's devotion?

#DontDoLifeAloneDevo #ReadPrayApplyRemain

2 Chronicles 24:1-25:28, Psalms 22:19-31, Proverbs 20:8-10, Romans 12:1-21

July 30

"Surely goodness and mercy shall follow me all the days of my life; And I will dwell in the house of the Lord Forever."
Psalms 23:6

Goodness and mercy are a byproduct of trusting the Lord and letting Him take the lead. Our great Shepherd knows where we need to go and what we need to get there. We can trust Him.

Thank you God for another day and for your word. Help me process it, live it and share it. In Jesus' name I pray, amen.

What is God speaking to you? What action will you take in light of today's devotion?

#DontDoLifeAloneDevo #ReadPrayApplyRemain

2 Chronicles 26:1-28:27, Psalms 23:1-6, Proverbs 20:11, Romans 13:1-14

July 31

"The earth is the Lord's, and all its fullness, The world and those who dwell therein."
Psalms 24:1

The creator of heaven and earth loves us. We can walk through life with confidence knowing that the one who made everything is mindful of us.

Thank you God for another day and for your word. Help me process it, live it and share it. In Jesus' name I pray, amen.

What is God speaking to you? Wha action will you take in light of today's devotion?

#DontDoLifeAloneDevo #ReadPrayApplyRemain

2 Chronicles 29:1-36, Psalms 24:1-10, Proverbs 20:1, Romans 14:1-23

August 1

"Now may the God of hope fill you with all joy and peace in believing, that you may abound in hope by the power of the Holy Spirit." Romans 15:13

When you run out of gas you go and get more from the gas station. Far too often, spiritually, we run on empty because we try to get filled up from sources that continually leave us empty. Let God fill you up today.

Thank you God for another day and for your word. Help me process it, live it and share it. In Jesus' name I pray, amen.

What is God speaking to you? What action will you take in light of today's devotion?

#DontDoLifeAloneDevo #ReadPrayApplyRemain

2 Chronicles 30:1-31:21, Psalms 25:1-15, Proverbs 20:13-15, Romans 15:1-22

August 2

"Let integrity and uprightness preserve me, for I wait for You." Psalms 25:21

While we are waiting for a breakthrough we can grow weary and frustrated. When we grow weary it's easier to lose track of what's important. Seek God and keep doing what's right in the Lord's sight and watch Him work.

Thank you God for another day and for your word. Help me process it, live it and share it. In Jesus' name I pray, amen.

What is God speaking to you? What action will you take in light of today's devotion?

#DontDoLifeAloneDevo #ReadPrayApplyRemain

2 Chronicles 32:1-33:13, Psalms 25:16-22, Proverbs 20:16-18, Romans 15:23-16:9

August 3

"I urge you, brothers and sisters, to watch out for those who cause divisions and put obstacles in your way that are contrary to the teaching you have learned. Keep away from them." Romans 16:17

If the enemy can keep us distracted and divided, we will miss out on opportunities to experience all that God has for us. This is true in every relationship. Do not give any space for the enemy to work.

Thank you God for another day and for your word. Help me process it, live it and share it. In Jesus' name I pray, amen.

What is God speaking to you? What action will you take in light of today's devotion?

#DontDoLifeAloneDevo #ReadPrayApplyRemain

2 Chronicles 33:14-34:33, Psalms 26:1-12, Proverbs 20:19, Romans 16:10-27

August 4

"For in the time of trouble He shall hide me in His pavilion; In the secret place of His tabernacle He shall hide me; He shall set me high upon a rock." Psalms 27:5

When things are overwhelming it is great to have a refuge to run to. We can't stick our heads in the sand every time things don't go our way, but everyone needs a place to rest and recharge. God is ready when you are.

Thank you God for another day and for your word. Help me process it, live it and share it. In Jesus' name I pray, amen.

What is God speaking to you? What action will you take in light of today's devotion?

#DontDoLifeAloneDevo #ReadPrayApplyRemain

2 Chronicles 35:1-36:23, Psalms 27:1-6, Proverbs 20:20-21, 1 Corinthians 1:1-17

August 5

"But God has chosen the foolish things of the world to put to shame the wise, and God has chosen the weak things of the world to put to shame the things which are mighty." I Corinthians 1:27

Many people struggle with feeling qualified to do anything for God. He has always used ordinary people to do extraordinary things and He created us for so much more.

Thank you God for another day and for your word. Help me process it, live it and share it. In Jesus' name I pray, amen.

What is God speaking to you? What action will you take in light of today's devotion?

#DontDoLifeAloneDevo #ReadPrayApplyRemain

Ezra 1:1-2:70, Psalms 27:7-14, Proverbs 20:22-23, 1 Corinthians 1:18-2:5

August 6

"But as it is written: "Eye has not seen, nor ear heard, nor have entered into the heart of man the things which God has prepared for those who love Him."" I Corinthians 2:9

We can experience the goodness of God now, but He has so much more in store! This world may have some things to offer, but they are nothing compared to what God has for you. Don't settle.

Thank you God for another day and for your word. Help me process it, live it and share it. In Jesus' name I pray, amen.

What is God speaking to you? What action will you take in light of today's devotion?

#DontDoLifeAloneDevo #ReadPrayApplyRemain

Ezra 3:1-4:23, Psalms 28:1-9, Proverbs 20:24-25, 1 Corinthians 2:6-3:4

August 7

"Let no one deceive himself. If anyone among you seems to be wise in this age, let him become a fool that he may become wise." I Corinthians 3:18

We have been blessed with the ability to learn and grow, but God is our greatest teacher. Let Him lead you and you will walk in grace and wisdom far beyond your own capacity.

Thank you God for another day and for your word. Help me process it, live it and share it. In Jesus' name I pray, amen.

What is God speaking to you? What action will you take in light of today's devotion?

#DontDoLifeAloneDevo #ReadPrayApplyRemain

Ezra 4:24-6:22, Psalms 29:1-11, Proverbs 20:26-27, 1 Corinthians 3:5-23

August 8

"Moreover it is required in stewards that one be found faithful." I Corinthians 4:2

Whether it is wisdom, time, resources or relationships, everything that God puts in our hands is a blessing. Let's steward it well and make the most of it.

Thank you God for another day and for your word. Help me process it, live it and share it. In Jesus' name I pray, amen.

What is God speaking to you? What action will you take in light of today's devotion?

#DontDoLifeAloneDevo #ReadPrayApplyRemain

Ezra 7:1-8:20, Psalms 30:1-12, Proverbs 20:28-30, 1 Corinthians 4:1-21

August 9

"And now for a little while grace has been shown from the LORD our God, to leave us a remnant to escape, and to give us a peg in His holy place, that our God may enlighten our eyes and give us a measure of revival in our bondage." Ezra 9:8

Even when things look hopeless, God is at work. Whatever we magnify gets bigger. Focus on the Lord and the pain and struggles of this world will grow strangely dim.

Thank you God for another day and for your word. Help me process it, live it and share it. In Jesus' name I pray, amen.

What is God speaking to you? What action will you take in light of today's devotion?

#DontDoLifeAloneDevo #ReadPrayApplyRemain

Ezra 8:21-9:15, Psalms 31:1-8, Proverbs 21:1-2, 1 Corinthians 5:1-13

August 10

"All things are lawful for me, but all things are not helpful. All things are lawful for me, but I will not be brought under the power of any." I Corinthians 6:12

Some things feel good in the moment but they do more harm than good. Ask the Lord for wisdom. Some decisions will keep you longer than you planned to stay and cost you more than you wanted to pay.

Thank you God for another day and for your word. Help me process it, live it and share it. In Jesus' name I pray, amen.

What is God speaking to you? What action will you take in light of today's devotion?

#DontDoLifeAloneDevo #ReadPrayApplyRemain

Ezra 10:1-44, Psalms 31:9-18, Proverbs 21:3, 1 Corinthians 6:1-20

August 11

"And I said to the king, "If it pleases the king, and if your servant has found favor in your sight, I ask that you send me to Judah, to the city of my fathers' tombs, that I may rebuild it.""
Nehemiah 2:5

Nehemiah had a burden for Judah, but he didn't just cry over the problem or complain about it. Nehemiah wanted things to change and he was willing to step up and do something about it. What need is in front of you that you can do something about?

Thank you God for another day and for your word. Help me process it, live it and share it. In Jesus' name I pray, amen.

What is God speaking to you? What action will you take in light of today's devotion?

#DontDoLifeAloneDevo #ReadPrayApplyRemain

Nehemiah 1:1-3:14, Psalms 31:19-24, Proverbs 21:4, 1 Corinthians 7:1-24

August 12

"The plans of the diligent lead surely to plenty, but those of everyone who is hasty, surely to poverty." Proverbs 21:5

When you are focused on the Lord and willing to work hard, there are no limitations. Shortcuts don't always lead you to your destination. Commit and stay the course.

Thank you God for another day and for your word. Help me process it, live it and share it. In Jesus' name I pray, amen.

What is God speaking to you? What action will you take in light of today's devotion?

#DontDoLifeAloneDevo #ReadPrayApplyRemain

Nehemiah 3:15-5:13, Psalms 32:1-11, Proverbs 21:5-7, 1 Corinthians 7:25-40

August 13

"So I sent messengers to them, saying, "I am doing a great work, so that I cannot come down. Why should the work cease while I leave it and go down to you?"" Nehemiah 6:3

If the enemy cannot deter you from walking out God's plan for your life, he will try to distract you. How you respond is up to you, but Nehemiah chose to not lose sight of the goal. You don't have to either.

Thank you God for another day and for your word. Help me process it, live it and share it. In Jesus' name I pray, amen.

What is God speaking to you? What action will you take in light of today's devotion?

#DontDoLifeAloneDevo #ReadPrayApplyRemain

Nehemiah 5:14-7:72, Psalms 33:1-11, Proverbs 21:8-10, 1 Corinthians 8:1-13

August 14

"Our soul waits for the LORD; He is our help and our shield." Psalms 33:20

Stop trying to fix your situation by yourself. Put it in God's hands and wait for Him to lead you. If you don't know what to do next, do whatever He told you to do last.

Thank you God for another day and for your word. Help me process it, live it and share it. In Jesus' name I pray, amen.

What is God speaking to you? What action will you take in light of today's devotion?

#DontDoLifeAloneDevo #ReadPrayApplyRemain

Nehemiah 7:73-9:21, Psalms 33:12-22, Proverbs 21:11-12, 1 Corinthians 9:1-18

August 15

"Do you not know that those who run in a race all run, but one receives the prize? Run in such a way that you may obtain it." I Corinthians 9:24

It is good to start off well, but that does not matter if you don't finish well. Don't worry about anyone else's race. Focus forward in humility, keep your heart pure, and let God lead the way.

Thank you God for another day and for your word. Help me process it, live it and share it. In Jesus' name I pray, amen.

What is God speaking to you? What action will you take in light of today's devotion?

#DontDoLifeAloneDevo #ReadPrayApplyRemain

Nehemiah 9:22-10:39, Psalms 34:1-10, Proverbs 21:13, 1 Corinthians 9:19-10:13

August 16

"The Lord is close to the brokenhearted and saves those who are crushed in spirit." Psalms 34:18

Regardless of the struggles that life may bring our way, God is more mindful of us than we realize. He is not limited by time, distance or our lack of understanding. He does His best work with broken people. Lean in and let Him love you.

Thank you God for another day and for your word. Help me process it, live it and share it. In Jesus' name I pray, amen.

What is God speaking to you? What action will you take in light of today's devotion?

#DontDoLifeAloneDevo #ReadPrayApplyRemain

Nehemiah 11:1-12:26, Psalms 34:11-22, Proverbs 21:14-16, 1 Corinthians 10:14-33

August 17

"And my soul shall be joyful in the LORD; It shall rejoice in His salvation." Psalms 35:9

Even when things are difficult there is something to be thankful for. If you have no other reason to rejoice, remember the cross and the price that Jesus paid to give us life. It's amazing!

Thank you God for another day and for your word. Help me process it, live it and share it. In Jesus' name I pray, amen.

What is God speaking to you? What action will you take in light of today's devotion?

#DontDoLifeAloneDevo #ReadPrayApplyRemain

Nehemiah 12:27-13:31, Psalms 35:1-16, Proverbs 21:17-18, 1 Corinthians 11:1-16

August 18

"And my tongue shall speak of Your righteousness and of Your praise all the day long." Psalms 35:28

Have you ever considered even just for one day all of the different things that you talk about? What would happen if our entire day was spent praising God? What gets our attention ultimately determines our direction.

Thank you God for another day and for your word. Help me process it, live it and share it. In Jesus' name I pray, amen.

What is God speaking to you? What action will you take in light of today's devotion?

#DontDoLifeAloneDevo #ReadPrayApplyRemain

Esther 1:1-3:15, Psalms 35:17-28, Proverbs 21:19-20, 1 Corinthians 11:17-34

August 19

"For if you remain completely silent at this time, relief and deliverance will arise for the Jews from another place, but you and your father's house will perish. Yet who knows whether you have come to the kingdom for such a time as this?" Esther 4:14

Mordecai was trying to help Esther understand that God had her where she was for a reason. Don't miss opportunities to do the things that God has prepared you for. God will work through you regardless of what is going on around you.

Thank you God for another day and for your word. Help me process it, live it and share it. In Jesus' name I pray, amen.

What is God speaking to you? What action will you take in light of today's devotion?

#DontDoLifeAloneDevo #ReadPrayApplyRemain

Esther 4:1-7:10, Psalms 36:1-12, Proverbs 21:21-22, 1 Corinthians 12:1-26

August 20

"Though I speak with the tongues of men and of angels, but have not love, I have become sounding brass or a clanging cymbal." I Corinthians 13:1

Words are powerful, but our actions speak louder than words. Love is not just a word that you share. Love is a way that you live. May our actions echo our words.

Thank you God for another day and for your word. Help me process it, live it and share it. In Jesus' name I pray, amen.

What is God speaking to you? What action will you take in light of today's devotion?

#DontDoLifeAloneDevo #ReadPrayApplyRemain

Esther 8:1-10:3, Psalms 37:1-11, Proverbs 21:23-24, 1 Corinthians 12:27-13:13

August 21

"And he said: "Naked I came from my mother's womb, and naked shall I return there. The LORD gave, and the LORD has taken away; Blessed be the name of the LORD."" Job 1:21

Even after Job had suffered from great losses, he still chose to praise God. Job decided that he was not going to allow his circumstances to dictate how he responded to God.

Thank you God for another day and for your word. Help me process it, live it and share it. In Jesus' name I pray, amen.

What is God speaking to you? What action will you take in light of today's devotion?

#DontDoLifeAloneDevo #ReadPrayApplyRemain

Job 1:1-3:26, Psalms 37:12-29, Proverbs 21:25-26, 1 Corinthians 14:1-17

August 22

"The mouth of the righteous speaks wisdom, and his tongue talks of justice." Psalms 37:30

You can tell a whole lot about a person by the subjects that they entertain and talk about. What or who do your words point to?

Thank you God for another day and for your word. Help me process it, live it and share it. In Jesus' name I pray, amen.

What is God speaking to you? What action will you take in light of today's devotion?

#DontDoLifeAloneDevo #ReadPrayApplyRemain

Job 4:1-7:21, Psalms 37:30-40, Proverbs 21:27, 1 Corinthians 14:18-40

August 23

"And your life would be brighter than noonday. Though you were dark, you would be like the morning." Job 11:1

Job's friends assumed that his pain was a result of sinful choices. Some people will judge you without knowing the full story, but that's okay. Stay true to the Lord and He will see you through.

Thank you God for another day and for your word. Help me process it, live it and share it. In Jesus' name I pray, amen.

What is God speaking to you? What action will you take in light of today's devotion?

#DontDoLifeAloneDevo #ReadPrayApplyRemain

Job 8:1-11:20, Psalms 38:1-22, Proverbs 21:28-29, 1 Corinthians 15:1-28

August 24

"Therefore, my beloved brethren, be steadfast, immovable, always abounding in the work of the Lord, knowing that your labor is not in vain in the Lord." I Corinthians 15:58

You can't stop a person that won't quit. Keep going! The pain and struggle that is being planted will eventually be the groundwork for a fruitful and fulfilling life.

Thank you God for another day and for your word. Help me process it, live it and share it. In Jesus' name I pray, amen.

What is God speaking to you? What action will you take in light of today's devotion?

#DontDoLifeAloneDevo #ReadPrayApplyRemain

Job 12:1-15:35, Psalms 39:1-13, Proverbs 21:30-31, 1 Corinthians 15:29-58

August 25

"For I know that my Redeemer lives, and He shall stand at last on the earth." Job 19:25

Even though Job's life seemed to be falling apart, he knew that he still had a redeemer. The storm may rage, but God is not done working in your story.

Thank you God for another day and for your word. Help me process it, live it and share it. In Jesus' name I pray, amen.

What is God speaking to you? What action will you take in light of today's devotion?

#DontDoLifeAloneDevo #ReadPrayApplyRemain

Job 16:1-19:29, Psalms 40:1-10, Proverbs 22:1, 1 Corinthians 16:1-24

August 26

"But I am poor and needy; Yet the LORD thinks upon me. You are my help and my deliverer; Do not delay, O my God." Psalms 40:17

God is more mindful of you than you realize. And regardless of what your need is, Jesus is always the solution. Trust Him.

Thank you God for another day and for your word. Help me process it, live it and share it. In Jesus' name I pray, amen.

What is God speaking to you? What action will you take in light of today's devotion?

#DontDoLifeAloneDevo #ReadPrayApplyRemain

Job 20:1-22:30, Psalms 40:11-17, Proverbs 22:2-4, 2 Corinthians 1:1-11

August 27

"For all the promises of God in Him are Yes, and in Him Amen, to the glory of God through us." II Corinthians 1:20

Just because you have not seen one of God's promises fulfilled, it does not mean you won't. The process is not on our timeline. Hold on.

Thank you God for another day and for your word. Help me process it, live it and share it. In Jesus' name I pray, amen.

What is God speaking to you? What action will you take in light of today's devotion?

#DontDoLifeAloneDevo #ReadPrayApplyRemain

Job 23:1-27:23, Psalms 41:1-13, Proverbs 22:5-6, 2 Corinthians 1:12-2:11

August 28

"Why, my soul, are you downcast? Why so disturbed within me? Put your hope in God, for I will yet praise him, my Savior and my God." Psalms 42:5

Some say that the greatest predictor of the future is the past. If there is any truth to that, God was faithful in the past, so we can trust Him now.

Thank you God for another day and for your word. Help me process it, live it and share it. In Jesus' name I pray, amen.

What is God speaking to you? What action will you take in light of today's devotion?

#DontDoLifeAloneDevo #ReadPrayApplyRemain

Job 28:1-30:31, Psalms 42:1-11, Proverbs 22:7, 2 Corinthians 2:12-17

August 29

"Now the Lord is the Spirit; and where the Spirit of the Lord is, there is liberty." 2 Corinthians 3:17

Many things promise freedom, but they don't deliver. It does not matter how big the burden is, nothing is too hard for God. Liberty is a byproduct of being in God's presence.

Thank you God for another day and for your word. Help me process it, live it and share it. In Jesus' name I pray, amen.

What is God speaking to you? What action will you take in light of today's devotion?

#DontDoLifeAloneDevo #ReadPrayApplyRemain

Job 31:1-33:33, Psalms 43:1-5, Proverbs 22:8-9, 2 Corinthians 3:1-18

August 30

"We are hard-pressed on every side, yet not crushed; we are perplexed, but not in despair."
2 Corinthians 4:8

Difficult circumstances can bring out the worst in us, but they can also bring out the best. When we are hard-pressed on every side, there is nothing to hide behind. Continue to lean in to Jesus, and He will see carry you.

Thank you God for another day and for your word. Help me process it, live it and share it. In Jesus' name I pray, amen.

What is God speaking to you? What action will you take in light of today's devotion?

#DontDoLifeAloneDevo #ReadPrayApplyRemain

Job 34:1-36:33, Psalms 44:1-8, Proverbs 22:10-12, 2 Corinthians 4:1-12

August 31

"While we do not look at the things which are seen, but at the things which are not seen. For the things which are seen are temporary, but the things which are not seen are eternal." 2 Corinthians 4:18

A friend that was recently diagnosed with cancer shared his new perspective about his life. He said that his presence on earth was for other people's benefit, but once his body was done the race, him getting to be with Jesus means he wins. Eternal perspective is not easy to grab a hold of, but our reward is not on this side of eternity.

Thank you God for another day and for your word. Help me process it, live it and share it. In Jesus' name I pray, amen.

What is God speaking to you? What action will you take in light of today's devotion?

#DontDoLifeAloneDevo #ReadPrayApplyRemain

Job 37:1-39:30, Psalms 44:9-26, Proverbs 22:13, 2 Corinthians 4:13-5:10

September 1

"And the LORD restored Job's losses when he prayed for his friends. Indeed the LORD gave Job twice as much as he had before." Job 42:10

The enemy had robbed Job of everything but his life. Because Job endured, God rewarded his faithfulness with restoration, two times over what he lost. Regardless of the struggle, hold on. God's got you covered.

Thank you God for another day and for your word. Help me process it, live it and share it. In Jesus' name I pray, amen.

What is God speaking to you? What action will you take in light of today's devotion?

#DontDoLifeAloneDevo #ReadPrayApplyRemain

Job 40:1-42:17, Psalms 45:1-17, Proverbs 22:14, 2 Corinthians 5:11-21

September 2

"The LORD of hosts is with us; The God of Jacob is our refuge. Selah" Psalms 46:11

One translation of the word Selah is a break in a song, or a pause. When you realize and recognize that God is with you, it will give you a chance to rest and catch your breath.

Thank you God for another day and for your word. Help me process it, live it and share it. In Jesus' name I pray, amen.

What is God speaking to you? What action will you take in light of today's devotion?

#DontDoLifeAloneDevo #ReadPrayApplyRemain

Ecclesiastes 1:1-3:22, Psalms 46:1-11, Proverbs 22:15, 2 Corinthians 6:1-13

September 3

"For if they fall, one will lift up his companion. But woe to him who is alone when he falls, for he has no one to help him up." Ecclesiastes 4:10

You may be one relationship away from a different life. Invest in life-giving relationships. Don't do life alone.

Thank you God for another day and for your word. Help me process it, live it and share it. In Jesus' name I pray, amen.

What is God speaking to you? What action will you take in light of today's devotion?

#DontDoLifeAloneDevo #ReadPrayApplyRemain

Ecclesiastes 4:1-6:12, Psalms 47:1-9, Proverbs 22:16, 2 Corinthians 6:14-7:7

September 4

"Wisdom strengthens the wise more than ten rulers of the city." Ecclesiastes 7:19

Some people think that their strength is found in what they do, but it may actually be found in what they can learn. We can never have enough wisdom. Keep growing.

Thank you God for another day and for your word. Help me process it, live it and share it. In Jesus' name I pray, amen.

What is God speaking to you? What action will you take in light of today's devotion?

#DontDoLifeAloneDevo #ReadPrayApplyRemain

Ecclesiastes 7:1-9:18, Psalms 48:1-14, Proverbs 22:17-19, 2 Corinthians 7:8-16

September 5

"If the ax is dull, and one does not sharpen the edge, then he must use more strength; But wisdom brings success." Ecclesiastes 10:10

Life is constantly changing, and we need to be as well. Don't just settle when things are not working out. Seek the Lord for direction and trust Him through it all.

Thank you God for another day and for your word. Help me process it, live it and share it. In Jesus' name I pray, amen.

What is God speaking to you? What action will you take in light of today's devotion?

#DontDoLifeAloneDevo #ReadPrayApplyRemain

Ecclesiastes 10:1-12:14, Psalms 49:1-20, Proverbs 22:20-21, 2 Corinthians 8:1-15

September 6

"Catch us the foxes, the little foxes that spoil the vines, for our vines have tender grapes." Song of Solomon 2:15

Just because something seems insignificant, it does not mean that it is. Little foxes spoil the vine. Pay attention and guard your heart. Little things can make a big difference for better or for worse.

Thank you God for another day and for your word. Help me process it, live it and share it. In Jesus' name I pray, amen.

What is God speaking to you? What action will you take in light of today's devotion?

#DontDoLifeAloneDevo #ReadPrayApplyRemain

Song of Solomon 1:1-4:16, Psalms 50:1-23, Proverbs 22:22-23, 2 Corinthians 8:16-24

September 7

"So let each one give as he purposes in his heart, not grudgingly or out of necessity; for God loves a cheerful giver." 2 Corinthians 9:7

We are blessed to be a blessing. Don't miss out on an opportunity to be generous or invest into something or someone that is making a difference.

Thank you God for another day and for your word. Help me process it, live it and share it. In Jesus' name I pray, amen.

What is God speaking to you? What action will you take in light of today's devotion?

#DontDoLifeAloneDevo #ReadPrayApplyRemain

Song of Solomon 5:1-8:14, Psalms 51:1-19, Proverbs 22:24-25, 2 Corinthians 9:1-15

September 8

"For though we walk in the flesh, we do not war according to the flesh." 2 Corinthians 10:3

Things are not always what they seem. Sometimes we need to take physical steps in order for things to change, but don't neglect the spiritual steps too. Pray first and let God take the lead.

Thank you God for another day and for your word. Help me process it, live it and share it. In Jesus' name I pray, amen.

What is God speaking to you? What action will you take in light of today's devotion?

#DontDoLifeAloneDevo #ReadPrayApplyRemain

Isaiah 1:1-2:22, Psalms 52:1-9, Proverbs 22:26-27, 2 Corinthians 10:1-18

September 9

"Do you see a man who excels in his work? He will stand before kings; He will not stand before unknown men." Proverbs 22:29

A lot of people waste time trying to get attention for what they do. Commit your work to the Lord and He will open doors and give you opportunities that you never could have created on your own.

Thank you God for another day and for your word. Help me process it, live it and share it. In Jesus' name I pray, amen.

What is God speaking to you? What action will you take in light of today's devotion?

#DontDoLifeAloneDevo #ReadPrayApplyRemain

Isaiah 3:1-5:30, Psalms 53:1-6, Proverbs 22:28-29, 2 Corinthians 11:1-15

September 10

"Also I heard the voice of the Lord, saying:
"Whom shall I send, and who will go for Us?"
Then I said, "Here am I! Send me."" Isaiah 6:8

God uses ordinary people to do extraordinary
things every single day. All that He is looking for
is a willing heart. Trust Him.

Thank you God for another day and for your
word. Help me process it, live it and share it. In
Jesus' name I pray, amen.

What is God speaking to you? What action will
you take in light of today's devotion?

#DontDoLifeAloneDevo #ReadPrayApplyRemain

Isaiah 6:1-7:25, Psalms 54:1-7, Proverbs 23:1-3,
2 Corinthians 11:16-33

September 11

"And He said to me, "My grace is sufficient for you, for My strength is made perfect in weakness." Therefore most gladly I will rather boast in my infirmities, that the power of Christ may rest upon me." 2 Corinthians 12:9

Far too often we lean on our own strength. When we are weak, He is strong. Lean in to Jesus and lay down your burdens.

Thank you God for another day and for your word. Help me process it, live it and share it. In Jesus' name I pray, amen.

What is God speaking to you? What action will you take in light of today's devotion?

#DontDoLifeAloneDevo #ReadPrayApplyRemain

Isaiah 8:1-9:21, Psalms 55:1-23, Proverbs 23:4-5, 2 Corinthians 12:1-10

September 12

"For as he thinks in his heart, so is he. "Eat and drink!" he says to you, But his heart is not with you." Proverbs 23:7

Our thinking impacts the direction that we are headed in. If you don't like where you are headed, renew your thoughts through prayer and God's word. Focus on Jesus first and watch things change.

Thank you God for another day and for your word. Help me process it, live it and share it. In Jesus' name I pray, amen.

What is God speaking to you? What action will you take in light of today's devotion?

#DontDoLifeAloneDevo #ReadPrayApplyRemain

Isaiah 10:1-11:16, Psalms 56:1-13, Proverbs 23:6-8, 2 Corinthians 12:11-21

September 13

"My heart is steadfast, O God, my heart is steadfast; I will sing and give praise." Psalms 57:7

Everything you do flows from your heart. Don't allow what may be wrong with you today, keep you from focusing on and worshipping what is right about God.

Thank you God for another day and for your word. Help me process it, live it and share it. In Jesus' name I pray, amen.

What is God speaking to you? What action will you take in light of today's devotion?

#DontDoLifeAloneDevo #ReadPrayApplyRemain

Isaiah 12:1-14:32, Psalms 57:1-11, Proverbs 23:9-11, 2 Corinthians 13:1-13

September 14

"For do I now persuade men, or God? Or do I seek to please men? For if I still pleased men, I would not be a bondservant of Christ."
Galatians 1:10

Pleasing God before we worry about others sounds good, but it is not always easy. The good news is, when we live to please God first, He will help us navigate all of our other relationships.

Thank you God for another day and for your word. Help me process it, live it and share it. In Jesus' name I pray, amen.

What is God speaking to you? What action will you take in light of today's devotion?

#DontDoLifeAloneDevo #ReadPrayApplyRemain

Isaiah 15:1-18:7, Psalms 58:1-11, Proverbs 23:12, Galatians 1:1-24

September 15

"I will wait for You, O You His strength; For God is my defense." Psalms 59:9

When we think of waiting for someone or something, inactivity often comes to mind. But what if we waited on God differently? What if we continued to wait on God like a waiter or waitress? Keep serving the Lord based on what He previously did until He speaks something different.

Thank you God for another day and for your word. Help me process it, live it and share it. In Jesus' name I pray, amen.

What is God speaking to you? What action will you take in light of today's devotion?

#DontDoLifeAloneDevo #ReadPrayApplyRemain

Isaiah 19:1-21:17, Psalms 59:1-17, Proverbs 23:13-14, Galatians 2:1-16

September 16

"I have been crucified with Christ; it is no longer I who live, but Christ lives in me; and the life which I now live in the flesh I live by faith in the Son of God, who loved me and gave Himself for me." Galatians 2:20

Our faith in Christ is not about checking off a box, or leaning on a thought process, or a particular way of life. Jesus loves you and me. He died for us! That's worth living for.

Thank you God for another day and for your word. Help me process it, live it and share it. In Jesus' name I pray, amen.

What is God speaking to you? What action will you take in light of today's devotion?

#DontDoLifeAloneDevo #ReadPrayApplyRemain

Isaiah 22:1-24:23, Psalms 60:1-12, Proverbs 23:15-16, Galatians 2:17-3:9

September 17

"You will keep him in perfect peace, Whose mind is stayed on You, Because he trusts in You." Isaiah 26:3

We can choose to focus on the problem or the solution. I may not always know what to do, but I know who does. Thankfully, the peace of God always surpasses my level of understanding.

Thank you God for another day and for your word. Help me process it, live it and share it. In Jesus' name I pray, amen.

What is God speaking to you? What action will you take in light of today's devotion?

#DontDoLifeAloneDevo #ReadPrayApplyRemain

Isaiah 25:1-28:13, Psalms 61:1-8, Proverbs 23:17-18, Galatians 3:10-22

September 18

"Therefore the Lord said: "In as much as these people draw near with their mouths and honor Me with their lips, but have removed their hearts far from Me, and their fear toward Me is taught by the commandment of men," Isaiah 29:13

God already knows the depths of our heart. He is not looking for a great performance. God loves you. He uniquely designed each of us to do incredible things! Just be the real you.

Thank you God for another day and for your word. Help me process it, live it and share it. In Jesus' name I pray, amen.

What is God speaking to you? What action will you take in light of today's devotion?

#DontDoLifeAloneDevo #ReadPrayApplyRemain

Isaiah 28:14-30:11, Psalms 62:1-12, Proverbs 23:19-21, Galatians 3:23-4:31

September 19

"Stand fast therefore in the liberty by which Christ has made us free, and do not be entangled again with a yoke of bondage."
Galatians 5:1

Jesus did not die on a cross to make bad people good. He died on a cross and rose again to bring spiritually dead people to life. So be free in Jesus name.

Thank you God for another day and for your word. Help me process it, live it and share it. In Jesus' name I pray, amen.

What is God speaking to you? What action will you take in light of today's devotion?

#DontDoLifeAloneDevo #ReadPrayApplyRemain

Isaiah 30:12-33:9, Psalms 63:1-11, Proverbs 23:22, Galatians 5:1-12

September 20

"Say to those who are fearful-hearted, "Be strong, do not fear! Behold, your God will come with vengeance, with the recompense of God; He will come and save you."" Isaiah 35:4

God does not always do things when we want or the way we want, but He is always there. We can go through life with peace knowing that regardless of what we are facing, we won't be facing it alone.

Thank you God for another day and for your word. Help me process it, live it and share it. In Jesus' name I pray, amen.

What is God speaking to you? What action will you take in light of today's devotion?

#DontDoLifeAloneDevo #ReadPrayApplyRemain

Isaiah 33:10-36:22, Psalms 64:1-10, Proverbs 23:23, Galatians 5:13-25

September 21

"And let us not grow weary while doing good, for in due season we shall reap if we do not lose heart." Galatians 6:9

Don't give up during a difficult chapter of your life. There are chapters yet to be written. God is not finished with your story.

Thank you God for another day and for your word. Help me process it, live it and share it. In Jesus' name I pray, amen.

What is God speaking to you? What action will you take in light of today's devotion?

#DontDoLifeAloneDevo #ReadPrayApplyRemain

Isaiah 37:1-38:22, Psalms 65:1-13, Proverbs 23:24, Galatians 6:1-18

September 22

"Fear not, for I am with you; Be not dismayed, for I am your God. I will strengthen you, Yes, I will help you, I will uphold you with My righteous right hand." Isaiah 41:10

Knowing that God has my back changes everything. He's not just another person to depend on. He is God and He is more mindful of us than we realize.

Thank you God for another day and for your word. Help me process it, live it and share it. In Jesus' name I pray, amen.

What is God speaking to you? What action will you take in light of today's devotion?

#DontDoLifeAloneDevo #ReadPrayApplyRemain

Isaiah 39:1-41:16, Psalms 66:1-20, Proverbs 23:25-28, Ephesians 1:1-23

September 23

"For we are His workmanship, created in Christ Jesus for good works, which God prepared beforehand that we should walk in them."
Ephesians 2:10

You are not an accident. You are called to live on purpose, with a purpose. You were created to do good things and equipped by God to create.

Thank you God for another day and for your word. Help me process it, live it and share it. In Jesus' name I pray, amen.

What is God speaking to you? What action will you take in light of today's devotion?

#DontDoLifeAloneDevo #ReadPrayApplyRemain

Isaiah 41:17-43:13, Psalms 67:1-7, Proverbs 23:29-35, Ephesians 2:1-22

September 24

"Now to Him who is able to do exceedingly abundantly above all that we ask or think, according to the power that works in us," Ephesians 3:20

Do not let fear, lack of resources or narrow opinions discourage you from dreaming big. Anything is possible when God is in the mix.

Thank you God for another day and for your word. Help me process it, live it and share it. In Jesus' name I pray, amen.

What is God speaking to you? What action will you take in light of today's devotion?

#DontDoLifeAloneDevo #ReadPrayApplyRemain

Isaiah 43:14-45:10, Psalms 68:1-18, Proverbs 24:1-2, Ephesians 3:1-21

September 25

"Through wisdom a house is built, and by understanding it is established;" Proverbs 24:3

There are a lot of different opinions and ideas about how we should live and build our life. We are over saturated with information, but it's not all beneficial. Seek God for wisdom and let him lead and help you build something that will last.

Thank you God for another day and for your word. Help me process it, live it and share it. In Jesus' name I pray, amen.

What is God speaking to you? What action will you take in light of today's devotion?

#DontDoLifeAloneDevo #ReadPrayApplyRemain

Isaiah 45:11-48:11, Psalms 68:19-35, Proverbs 24:3-4, Ephesians 4:1-16

September 26

"Do not let any unwholesome talk come out of your mouths, but only what is helpful for building others up according to their needs, that it may benefit those who listen." Ephesians 4:29

In the book of Proverbs we are reminded that life and death are in the power of the tongue. Choose to speak life. Build others up! The world already has enough hurtful and negative words being shared.

Thank you God for another day and for your word. Help me process it, live it and share it. In Jesus' name I pray, amen.

What is God speaking to you? What action will you take in light of today's devotion?

#DontDoLifeAloneDevo #ReadPrayApplyRemain

Isaiah 48:12-50:11, Psalms 69:1-18, Proverbs 24:5-6, Ephesians 4:17-32

September 27

"And walk in love, as Christ also has loved us and given Himself for us, an offering and a sacrifice to God for a sweet-smelling aroma." Ephesians 5:2

The best way to live like Jesus is to love like Jesus. It does not matter what else we do, if it's not done in love, we are missing it.

Thank you God for another day and for your word. Help me process it, live it and share it. In Jesus' name I pray, amen.

What is God speaking to you? What action will you take in light of today's devotion?

#DontDoLifeAloneDevo #ReadPrayApplyRemain

Isaiah 51:1-53:12, Psalms 69:19-36, Proverbs 24:7, Ephesians 5:1-33

September 28

""For as the heavens are higher than the earth, so are My ways higher than your ways, and My thoughts than your thoughts." Isaiah 55:9

Even on our best day, we still need the Lord to lead us. God knows what we need better than we do. We can trust Him.

Thank you God for another day and for your word. Help me process it, live it and share it. In Jesus' name I pray, amen.

What is God speaking to you? What action will you take in light of today's devotion?

#DontDoLifeAloneDevo #ReadPrayApplyRemain

Isaiah 54:1-57:14, Psalms 70:1-5, Proverbs 24:8, Ephesians 6:1-24

September 29

"Being confident of this very thing, that He who has begun a good work in you will complete it until the day of Jesus Christ;" Philippians 1:6

Regardless of what you may be facing and what chapter of life you may be walking through, God is not finished with your story.

Thank you God for another day and for your word. Help me process it, live it and share it. In Jesus' name I pray, amen.

What is God speaking to you? What action will you take in light of today's devotion?

#DontDoLifeAloneDevo #ReadPrayApplyRemain

Isaiah 57:15-59:21, Psalms 71:1-24, Proverbs 24:9-10, Philippians 1:1-26

September 30

"Do all things without complaining and disputing," Philippians 2:14

There are people praying for the things that we easily take for granted. There is plenty to be thankful for. Try to go a day without complaining about anything, and see how much better you feel.

Thank you God for another day and for your word. Help me process it, live it and share it. In Jesus' name I pray, amen.

What is God speaking to you? What action will you take in light of today's devotion?

#DontDoLifeAloneDevo #ReadPrayApplyRemain

Isaiah 60:1-62:5, Psalms 72:1-20, Proverbs 24:11-12, Philippians 1:27-2:18

October 1

"But now, O Lord, You are our Father; We are the clay, and You our potter; And all we are the work of Your hand." Isaiah 64:8

God is a redeemer. He uses us to impact others, and other things to help shape and impact us. The good news is, He is involved in the details of our life. And nothing is wasted.

Thank you God for another day and for your word. Help me process it, live it and share it. In Jesus' name I pray, amen.

What is God speaking to you? What action will you take in light of today's devotion?

#DontDoLifeAloneDevo #ReadPrayApplyRemain

Isaiah 62:6-65:25, Psalms 73:1-28, Proverbs 24:13-14, Philippians 2:19-3:3

October 2

"Brothers and sisters, I do not consider myself yet to have taken hold of it. But one thing I do: Forgetting what is behind and straining toward what is ahead," Philippians 3:13

Don't let the pain of the past steal your joy in the present or your hope for the future. God is not finished with your story. Your best days are ahead.

Thank you God for another day and for your word. Help me process it, live it and share it. In Jesus' name I pray, amen.

What is God speaking to you? What action will you take in light of today's devotion?

#DontDoLifeAloneDevo #ReadPrayApplyRemain

Isaiah 66:1-24, Psalms 74:1-23, Proverbs 24:15-16, Philippians 3:4-21

October 3

" "My people have committed two sins: They have forsaken me, the spring of living water, and have dug their own cisterns, broken cisterns that cannot hold water." Jeremiah 2:13

A broken cistern is a water well that can't hold water. Jesus is the only well that will never run dry. Stop trying to quench your thirst with broken wells.

Thank you God for another day and for your word. Help me process it, live it and share it. In Jesus' name I pray, amen.

What is God speaking to you? What action will you take in light of today's devotion?

#DontDoLifeAloneDevo #ReadPrayApplyRemain

Jeremiah 1:1-2:30, Psalms 75:1-10, Proverbs 24:17-20, Philippians 4:1-23

October 4

"That you may walk worthy of the Lord, fully pleasing Him, being fruitful in every good work and increasing in the knowledge of God;"
Colossians 1:10

Change is inevitable, but growth is optional. If you are going to go through it, grow through it. Nothing is wasted.

Thank you God for another day and for your word. Help me process it, live it and share it. In Jesus' name I pray, amen.

What is God speaking to you? What action will you take in light of today's devotion?

#DontDoLifeAloneDevo #ReadPrayApplyRemain

Jeremiah 2:31-4:18, Psalms 76:1-12, Proverbs 24:21-22, Colossians 1:1-17

October 5

"I will remember the works of the Lord; Surely I will remember Your wonders of old." Psalms 77:11

God has done so much! Sometimes God meets a need that we have been praying about, but we move on so quickly to what we need next, we forget about what He has already done. Take some time to reflect on the goodness of God today. Gratitude changes everything.

Thank you God for another day and for your word. Help me process it, live it and share it. In Jesus' name I pray, amen.

What is God speaking to you? What action will you take in light of today's devotion?

#DontDoLifeAloneDevo #ReadPrayApplyRemain

Jeremiah 4:19-6:15, Psalms 77:1-20, Proverbs 24:23-25, Colossians 1:18-2:7

October 6

"Thus says the Lord: "Stand in the ways and see, and ask for the old paths, where the good way is, and walk in it; Then you will find rest for your souls. But they said, 'We will not walk in it.'" Jeremiah 6:16

Our culture pushes us to pursue the latest and greatest. New things can be fun, or change things up, but sometimes they can also lead us in the wrong direction. God can do a new work in your life, even if the path to get there is not new. Let Him lead you.

Thank you God for another day and for your word. Help me process it, live it and share it. In Jesus' name I pray, amen.

What is God speaking to you? What action will you take in light of today's devotion?

#DontDoLifeAloneDevo #ReadPrayApplyRemain

Jeremiah 6:16-8:7, Psalms 78:1-31, Proverbs 24:26, Colossians 2:8-23

October 7

"And whatever you do in word or deed, do all in the name of the Lord Jesus, giving thanks to God the Father through Him." Colossians 3:17

When you choose to do what you do in Jesus name and in honor of the Lord, it changes how you work. Knowing your reason why is so important.

Thank you God for another day and for your word. Help me process it, live it and share it. In Jesus' name I pray, amen.

What is God speaking to you? What action will you take in light of today's devotion?

#DontDoLifeAloneDevo #ReadPrayApplyRemain

Jeremiah 8:8-9:26, Psalms 78:32-55, Proverbs 24:27, Colossians 3:1-17

October 8

"So he shepherded them according to the integrity of his heart, and guided them by the skillfulness of his hands." Psalms 78:72

God used David's experience as a shepherd to help him lead as the King of Israel. He will use your past and present to prepare you for your future. He's got you covered. Nothing is wasted.

Thank you God for another day and for your word. Help me process it, live it and share it. In Jesus' name I pray, amen.

What is God speaking to you? What action will you take in light of today's devotion?

#DontDoLifeAloneDevo #ReadPrayApplyRemain

Jeremiah 10:1-11:23, Psalms 78:56-72, Proverbs 24:28-29, Colossians 3:18-4:18

October 9

""If you have raced with men on foot and they have worn you out, how can you compete with horses? If you stumble in safe country, how will you manage in the thickets by the Jordan?"
Jeremiah 12:5

By design our brains are made to protect us and conserve energy, so it makes sense for us to prefer the path of least resistance. But sometimes we have to push through the hard things. If you find yourself on a difficult path, just make sure it's a path that you should be on. God will lead you.

Thank you God for another day and for your word. Help me process it, live it and share it. In Jesus' name I pray, amen.

What is God speaking to you? What action will you take in light of today's devotion?

#DontDoLifeAloneDevo #ReadPrayApplyRemain

Jeremiah 12:1-14:10, Psalms 79:1-13, Proverbs 24:30-34, 1 Thessalonians 1:1-2:8

October 10

"It is the glory of God to conceal a matter, but the glory of kings is to search out a matter." Proverbs 25:2

We can't see the radio waves flowing through the spaces that we occupy, but with the right radio tuner, we can tune in to a frequency to hear it. God is always communicating in some capacity, but we are not always listening. Seek the Lord, search out what He has for you, and slow down long enough to receive it.

Thank you God for another day and for your word. Help me process it, live it and share it. In Jesus' name I pray, amen.

What is God speaking to you? What action will you take in light of today's devotion?

#DontDoLifeAloneDevo #ReadPrayApplyRemain

Jeremiah 14:11-16:15, Psalms 80:1-9, Proverbs 25:1-5, 1 Thessalonians 2:9-3:13

October 11

"But blessed is the one who trusts in the Lord, whose confidence is in him." Jeremiah 17:7

We put our trust in a lot of things. Most things over promise but under deliver, but not God. He is who He said He is, and He will do what He said He would do. Trust Him.

Thank you God for another day and for your word. Help me process it, live it and share it. In Jesus' name I pray, amen.

What is God speaking to you? What action will you take in light of today's devotion?

#DontDoLifeAloneDevo #ReadPrayApplyRemain

Jeremiah 16:16-18:23, Psalms 81:1-16, Proverbs 25:6-8, 1 Thessalonians 4:1-5:3

October 12

"In everything give thanks; for this is the will of God in Christ Jesus for you." I Thessalonians 5:18

We can't experience all that God has for us without gratitude. God gave us another day. Let's live in response to this incredible gift that we call the present. Gratitude changes everything.

Thank you God for another day and for your word. Help me process it, live it and share it. In Jesus' name I pray, amen.

What is God speaking to you? What action will you take in light of today's devotion?

#DontDoLifeAloneDevo #ReadPrayApplyRemain

Jeremiah 19:1-21:14, Psalms 82:1-8, Proverbs 25:9-10, 1 Thessalonians 5:4-28

October 13

"A word fitly spoken is like apples of gold In settings of silver." Proverbs 25:11

How do you know for certain if someone nearby needs encouragement? If they are still breathing. Speak life! A few words of encouragement from you could be the thing that makes their life better today.

Thank you God for another day and for your word. Help me process it, live it and share it. In Jesus' name I pray, amen.

What is God speaking to you? What action will you take in light of today's devotion?

#DontDoLifeAloneDevo #ReadPrayApplyRemain

Jeremiah 22:1-23:20, Psalms 83:1-18, Proverbs 25:11-14, 2 Thessalonians 1:1-12

October 14

"For a day in Your courts is better than a thousand. I would rather be a doorkeeper in the house of my God than dwell in the tents of wickedness." Psalms 84:10

Holding the door for people may seem like a simple task, but it's not insignificant. Knowing that you are in proximity to God is a blessing. Holding the door for other people to experience the love of God is an even greater blessing.

Thank you God for another day and for your word. Help me process it, live it and share it. In Jesus' name I pray, amen.

What is God speaking to you? What action will you take in light of today's devotion?

#DontDoLifeAloneDevo #ReadPrayApplyRemain

Jeremiah 23:21-25:38, Psalms 84:1-12, Proverbs 25:15, 2 Thessalonians 2:1-17

October 15

"And as for you, brothers and sisters, never tire of doing what is good." 2 Thessalonians 3:13

At times doing the right thing or a good thing can also be a hard thing. But God honors faith and obedience. When the good thing is a God thing, He will bless you. Keep on keeping on.

Thank you God for another day and for your word. Help me process it, live it and share it. In Jesus' name I pray, amen.

What is God speaking to you? What action will you take in light of today's devotion?

#DontDoLifeAloneDevo #ReadPrayApplyRemain

Jeremiah 26:1-27:22, Psalms 85:1-13, Proverbs 25:16, 2 Thessalonians 3:1-18

October 16

"And you will seek Me and find Me, when you search for Me with all your heart." Jeremiah 29:13

There are a lot of things in life that we focus on and pursue that will only satisfy temporarily, but God is a well that will never run dry. He's ready when you are.

Thank you God for another day and for your word. Help me process it, live it and share it. In Jesus' name I pray, amen.

What is God speaking to you? What action will you take in light of today's devotion?

#DontDoLifeAloneDevo #ReadPrayApplyRemain

Jeremiah 28:1-29:32, Psalms 86:1-17, Proverbs 25:17, 1 Timothy 1:1-20

October 17

"There is hope in your future, says the Lord, That your children shall come back to their own border." Jeremiah 31:17

God is speaking to the children of Israel in this verse, but that promise is not just true for them. The breath in your lungs and heart beating in your chest while you are reading this is a reminder that there is hope in your future and that God is clearly not finished with your story.

Thank you God for another day and for your word. Help me process it, live it and share it. In Jesus' name I pray, amen.

What is God speaking to you? What action will you take in light of today's devotion?

#DontDoLifeAloneDevo #ReadPrayApplyRemain

Jeremiah 30:1-31:26, Psalms 87:1-7, Proverbs 25:18-19, 1 Timothy 2:1-15

October 18

"If your enemy is hungry, give him bread to eat;
And if he is thirsty, give him water to drink;
Proverbs 25:21

God tells us to bless people that we don't
necessarily get along with. That may be counter
to how we feel, but most of what God calls us to
do is different than what our flesh or other
people think we should do.

Thank you God for another day and for your
word. Help me process it, live it and share it. In
Jesus' name I pray, amen.

What is God speaking to you? What action will
you take in light of today's devotion?

#DontDoLifeAloneDevo #ReadPrayApplyRemain

Jeremiah 31:27-32:44, Psalms 88:1-18, Proverbs
25:20-22, 1 Timothy 3:1-16

October 19

"Let no one despise your youth, but be an example to the believers in word, in conduct, in love, in spirit, in faith, in purity." I Timothy 4:12

God does not waste any season of our life. If you are young, listen to people that have gone on before you. If you are older, invest in people that are coming up behind you. Take the meat and spit out the bones. Hold on to what is good, let go of the rest, and make the moments count.

Thank you God for another day and for your word. Help me process it, live it and share it. In Jesus' name I pray, amen.

What is God speaking to you? What action will you take in light of today's devotion?

#DontDoLifeAloneDevo #ReadPrayApplyRemain

Jeremiah 33:1-34:22, Psalms 89:1-13, Proverbs 25:23-24, 1 Timothy 4:1-16

October 20

"As cold water to a weary soul, so is good news from a far country." Proverbs 25:25

Every single day we are given opportunities to speak into peoples lives. With our words we can refresh or discourage. We can share good news or negativity. We don't always get it right, but do your best to speak life!

Thank you God for another day and for your word. Help me process it, live it and share it. In Jesus' name I pray, amen.

What is God speaking to you? What action will you take in light of today's devotion?

#DontDoLifeAloneDevo #ReadPrayApplyRemain

Jeremiah 35:1-36:32, Psalms 89:14-37, Proverbs 25:25-27, 1 Timothy 5:1-25

October 21

"Fight the good fight of faith, lay hold on eternal life, to which you were also called and have confessed the good confession in the presence of many witnesses." I Timothy 6:12

There are seasons of life where everything feels like an uphill battle. The good news is, we have so much to look forward to. Don't give up along the way.

Thank you God for another day and for your word. Help me process it, live it and share it. In Jesus' name I pray, amen.

What is God speaking to you? What action will you take in light of today's devotion?

#DontDoLifeAloneDevo #ReadPrayApplyRemain

Jeremiah 37:1-38:28, Psalms 89:38-52, Proverbs 25:28, 1 Timothy 6:1-21

October 22

"For God has not given us a spirit of fear, but of power and of love and of a sound mind." 2 Timothy 1:7

Fear is not a fruit of the spirit and it does not get to have the final say in your life. God is for you and that is more than enough. Let His power and love help you push through the fear that tries to hold you back.

Thank you God for another day and for your word. Help me process it, live it and share it. In Jesus' name I pray, amen.

What is God speaking to you? What action will you take in light of today's devotion?

#DontDoLifeAloneDevo #ReadPrayApplyRemain

Jeremiah 39:1-41:18, Psalms 90:1-91:16, Proverbs 26:1-2, 2 Timothy 1:1-18

October 23

"Those who are planted in the house of the Lord shall flourish in the courts of our God." Psalms 92:13

To be planted means to be connected. Being planted in the house of the Lord connects us to God, community and a faith that changes how we walk through life. That's a pretty amazing offer.

Thank you God for another day and for your word. Help me process it, live it and share it. In Jesus' name I pray, amen.

What is God speaking to you? What action will you take in light of today's devotion?

#DontDoLifeAloneDevo #ReadPrayApplyRemain

Jeremiah 42:1-44:23, Psalms 92:1-93:5, Proverbs 26:3-5, 2 Timothy 2:1-21

October 24

"But avoid foolish and ignorant disputes, knowing that they generate strife." 2 Timothy 2:23

Conversations that do nothing but create conflict are a waste of time and can do damage to our relationships. We can still love people well even if we don't agree on everything, but we don't need to argue with them.

Thank you God for another day and for your word. Help me process it, live it and share it. In Jesus' name I pray, amen.

What is God speaking to you? What action will you take in light of today's devotion?

#DontDoLifeAloneDevo #ReadPrayApplyRemain

Jeremiah 44:24-47:7, Psalms 94:1-23, Proverbs 26:6-8, 2 Timothy 2:22-3:17

October 25

"I have fought the good fight, I have finished the race, I have kept the faith." 2 Timothy 4:7

I know plenty of people that started off well, but they did not finish well. When it comes to my faith, or how I love and steward my family, relationships, time, talent, calling or resources, I pray that one day I too can say that I have fought the good fight, finished the race, and kept the faith.

Thank you God for another day and for your word. Help me process it, live it and share it. In Jesus' name I pray, amen.

What is God speaking to you? What action will you take in light of today's devotion?

#DontDoLifeAloneDevo #ReadPrayApplyRemain

Jeremiah 48:1-49:22, Psalms 95:1-96:13, Proverbs 26:9-12, 2 Timothy 4:1-22

October 26

"Light shines on the godly, and joy on those whose hearts are right." Psalms 97:11

One of the pastors at our church often talks about God working downstream. We can't earn grace, but there is a direct correlation between some blessings and our obedience.

Thank you God for another day and for your word. Help me process it, live it and share it. In Jesus' name I pray, amen.

What is God speaking to you? What action will you take in light of today's devotion?

#DontDoLifeAloneDevo #ReadPrayApplyRemain

Jeremiah 49:23-50:46, Psalms 97:1-98:9, Proverbs 26:13-16, Titus 1:1-16

October 27

"Like one who grabs a stray dog by the ears is someone who rushes into a quarrel not their own." Proverbs 26:17

We can pray and trust God to move in a situation without getting involved in something that could create more issues. Always pray first. God will lead you.

Thank you God for another day and for your word. Help me process it, live it and share it. In Jesus' name I pray, amen.

What is God speaking to you? What action will you take in light of today's devotion?

#DontDoLifeAloneDevo #ReadPrayApplyRemain

Jeremiah 51:1-53, Psalms 99:1-9, Proverbs 26:17, Titus 2:1-15

October 28

"Enter into His gates with thanksgiving, and into His courts with praise. Be thankful to Him, and bless His name." Psalms 100:4

We can spend so much time dwelling on what we want or need that we quickly dismiss what God has already done. Things don't have to be perfect or even great in order for us to be thankful for the goodness of God in our life.

Thank you God for another day and for your word. Help me process it, live it and share it. In Jesus' name I pray, amen.

What is God speaking to you? What action will you take in light of today's devotion?

#DontDoLifeAloneDevo #ReadPrayApplyRemain

Jeremiah 51:54-52:34, Psalms 100:1-5, Proverbs 26:18-19, Titus 3:1-15

October 29

"Where there is no wood, the fire goes out; And where there is no talebearer, strife ceases."
Proverbs 26:20

Fuel what matters. Some conversations need to end, while others need to continue. Invest in things that are worth your time and energy. Let God lead you.

Thank you God for another day and for your word. Help me process it, live it and share it. In Jesus' name I pray, amen.

What is God speaking to you? What action will you take in light of today's devotion?

#DontDoLifeAloneDevo #ReadPrayApplyRemain

Lamentations 1:1-2:22, Psalms 101:1-8, Proverbs 26:20, Philemon 1:1-25

October 30

"Through the Lord's mercies we are not consumed, because His compassions fail not." Lamentations 3:22

Are you living your life in a way that makes the most of every day? If not, today is a great day to start. God's mercies are new every morning. Today is a gift. It's called the present. Let's not take it for granted.

Thank you God for another day and for your word. Help me process it, live it and share it. In Jesus' name I pray, amen.

What is God speaking to you? What action will you take in light of today's devotion?

#DontDoLifeAloneDevo #ReadPrayApplyRemain

Lamentations 3:1-66, Psalms 102:1-28, Proverbs 26:21-22, Hebrews 1:1-14

October 31

"Bless the Lord, O my soul, and forget not all His benefits:" Psalms 103:2

Someone else is praying for the things that you and I sometimes take for granted. Gratitude changes everything. Don't forget to stop and say thank you for all of the amazing things that God has done in your life.

Thank you God for another day and for your word. Help me process it, live it and share it. In Jesus' name I pray, amen.

What is God speaking to you? What action will you take in light of today's devotion?

#DontDoLifeAloneDevo #ReadPrayApplyRemain

Lamentations 4:1-5:22, Psalms 103:1-22, Proverbs 26:23, Hebrews 2:1-18

November 1

"He appointed the moon for seasons; The sun knows its going down." Psalms 104:19

Five minutes ago the sky looked completely different then it does right now. Much like life, it can change very quickly. I'm thankful that the one who paints the sky is more mindful of us than we realize, and when everything else is changing, God remains faithful.

Thank you God for another day and for your word. Help me process it, live it and share it. In Jesus' name I pray, amen.

What is God speaking to you? What action will you take in light of today's devotion?

#DontDoLifeAloneDevo #ReadPrayApplyRemain

Ezekiel 1:1-3:15, Psalms 104:1-23, Proverbs 26:24-26, Hebrews 3:1-19

November 2

"For the word of God is living and powerful, and sharper than any two-edged sword, piercing even to the division of soul and spirit, and of joints and marrow, and is a discerner of the thoughts and intents of the heart." Hebrews 4:12

There are some books that you read and they impact your life, but none quite like the book of books that we call the Bible. You can read it now, and in a different season of your life read the same scripture and it will speak to you in a different way. Keep reading. It gets better.

Thank you God for another day and for your word. Help me process it, live it and share it. In Jesus' name I pray, amen.

What is God speaking to you? What action will you take in light of today's devotion?

#DontDoLifeAloneDevo #ReadPrayApplyRemain

Ezekiel 3:16-6:14, Psalms 104:24-35, Proverbs 26:27, Hebrews 4:1-16

November 3

"Oh, give thanks to the Lord! Call upon His name; Make known His deeds among the peoples!" Psalms 105:1

When God does something in your life, tell somebody. We pray for God to move, but when He does, we quickly move on to the next thing we need. Other people need to hear good news too. Talk about your testimonies.

Thank you God for another day and for your word. Help me process it, live it and share it. In Jesus' name I pray, amen.

What is God speaking to you? What action will you take in light of today's devotion?

#DontDoLifeAloneDevo #ReadPrayApplyRemain

Ezekiel 7:1-9:11, Psalms 105:1-15, Proverbs 26:28, Hebrews 5:1-14

November 4

"Do not boast about tomorrow, for you do not know what a day may bring forth." Proverbs 27:1

Life can change quickly and tomorrow is not promised. Plan for forever, but make today count. Love well, forgive quickly and make the most of the moments.

Thank you God for another day and for your word. Help me process it, live it and share it. In Jesus' name I pray, amen.

What is God speaking to you? What action will you take in light of today's devotion?

#DontDoLifeAloneDevo #ReadPrayApplyRemain

Ezekiel 10:1-11:25, Psalms 105:16-36, Proverbs 27:1-2, Hebrews 6:1-20

November 5

"He opened the rock, and water gushed out; It ran in the dry places like a river." Psalms 105:41

God will provide and sometimes He will use unconventional ways to do so. Don't close your mind off to how things could happen. Just trust Him.

Thank you God for another day and for your word. Help me process it, live it and share it. In Jesus' name I pray, amen.

What is God speaking to you? What action will you take in light of today's devotion?

#DontDoLifeAloneDevo #ReadPrayApplyRemain

Ezekiel 12:1-14:11, Psalms 105:37-45, Proverbs 27:3, Hebrews 7:1-17

November 6

"Faithful are the wounds of a friend, but the kisses of an enemy are deceitful." Proverbs 27:6

When a difficult conversation in hopes of making something better is needed, some people refer to it as tough love. It's actually just love. When you genuinely care about someone you will tell them the truth, even when that in itself is difficult.

Thank you God for another day and for your word. Help me process it, live it and share it. In Jesus' name I pray, amen.

What is God speaking to you? What action will you take in light of today's devotion?

#DontDoLifeAloneDevo #ReadPrayApplyRemain

Ezekiel 14:12-16:41, Psalms 106:1-12, Proverbs 27:4-6, Hebrews 7:18-28

November 7

"They soon forgot His works; They did not wait for His counsel," Psalms 106:13

This scripture starts with the word they, but if we are not careful we will repeat the same pattern. God has been so good to us. He is still worth remembering and trusting.

Thank you God for another day and for your word. Help me process it, live it and share it. In Jesus' name I pray, amen.

What is God speaking to you? What action will you take in light of today's devotion?

#DontDoLifeAloneDevo #ReadPrayApplyRemain

Ezekiel 16:42-17:24, Psalms 106:13-31, Proverbs 27:7-9, Hebrews 8:1-13

November 8

"Do not forsake your own friend or your father's friend, nor go to your brother's house in the day of your calamity; Better is a neighbor nearby than a brother far away." Proverbs 27:10

Jesus said that people will know that we follow Him because of our love. God called us to love our neighbor as ourselves. One of the best ways to do that is to be present and willing to serve.

Thank you God for another day and for your word. Help me process it, live it and share it. In Jesus' name I pray, amen.

What is God speaking to you? What action will you take in light of today's devotion?

#DontDoLifeAloneDevo #ReadPrayApplyRemain

Ezekiel 18:1-19:14, Psalms 106:32-48, Proverbs 27:10, Hebrews 9:1-10

November 9

"Let the redeemed of the Lord say so, whom He has redeemed from the hand of the enemy," Psalms 107:2

I don't think it's possible to hear redemption stories enough. If God has done something in your life today, this week, this month or even if you have to throw it way back, tell somebody!

Thank you God for another day and for your word. Help me process it, live it and share it. In Jesus' name I pray, amen.

What is God speaking to you? What action will you take in light of today's devotion?

#DontDoLifeAloneDevo #ReadPrayApplyRemain

Ezekiel 20:1-49, Psalms 107:1-43, Proverbs 27:11, Hebrews 9:11-28

November 10

"For Your mercy is great above the heavens, and Your truth reaches to the clouds." Psalms 108:4

The mercy that people offer come with limits, but God's love and mercy have no bounds. When you look up to the sky, do so with gratitude. We are far better off than we deserve.

Thank you God for another day and for your word. Help me process it, live it and share it. In Jesus' name I pray, amen.

What is God speaking to you? What action will you take in light of today's devotion?

#DontDoLifeAloneDevo #ReadPrayApplyRemain

Ezekiel 21:1-22:31, Psalms 108:1-13, Proverbs 27:12, Hebrews 10:1-17

November 11

"Let us hold fast the confession of our hope without wavering, for He who promised is faithful." Hebrews 10:23

There are a lot of people that make promises but don't ever follow through. It's great to be able to put your trust in a God who makes good on His word.

Thank you God for another day and for your word. Help me process it, live it and share it. In Jesus' name I pray, amen.

What is God speaking to you? What action will you take in light of today's devotion?

#DontDoLifeAloneDevo #ReadPrayApplyRemain

Ezekiel 23:1-49, Psalms 109:1-31, Proverbs 27:13, Hebrews 10:18-39

November 12

"But without faith it is impossible to please Him, for he who comes to God must believe that He is, and that He is a rewarder of those who diligently seek Him." Hebrews 11:6

Fear of failure will hold us back more than the pain of regret ever will. Walking by faith is not always easy, but it will always be worth it.

Thank you God for another day and for your word. Help me process it, live it and share it. In Jesus' name I pray, amen.

What is God speaking to you? What action will you take in light of today's devotion?

#DontDoLifeAloneDevo #ReadPrayApplyRemain

Ezekiel 24:1-26:21, Psalms 110:1-7, Proverbs 27:14, Hebrews 11:1-16

November 13

"He has sent redemption to His people; He has commanded His covenant forever: Holy and awesome is His name." Psalms 111:9

As a child our grandmother always encouraged us to count our blessings. I really try, but I can't count that high. Even when everything is not great, I am still far better off than I deserve, and all because of the goodness of God.

Thank you God for another day and for your word. Help me process it, live it and share it. In Jesus' name I pray, amen.

What is God speaking to you? What action will you take in light of today's devotion?

#DontDoLifeAloneDevo #ReadPrayApplyRemain

Ezekiel 27:1-28:26, Psalms 111:1-10, Proverbs 27:15-16, Hebrews 11:17-31

November 14

"Looking unto Jesus, the author and finisher of our faith, who for the joy that was set before Him endured the cross, despising the shame, and has sat down at the right hand of the throne of God." Hebrews 12:2

God believes in you when others don't. God sees your potential when others can't. You can trust Him with editorial control of your life.

Thank you God for another day and for your word. Help me process it, live it and share it. In Jesus' name I pray, amen.

What is God speaking to you? What action will you take in light of today's devotion?

#DontDoLifeAloneDevo #ReadPrayApplyRemain

Ezekiel 29:1-30:26, Psalms 112:1-10, Proverbs 27:17, Hebrews 11:32-12:13

November 15

"As water reflects the face, so one's life reflects the heart." Proverbs 27:19

If you want to know who someone really is, pay attention to what they say and do. If you want what you say and do to change, do the heart work. The heart work can be hard word, but it's worth it.

Thank you God for another day and for your word. Help me process it, live it and share it. In Jesus' name I pray, amen.

What is God speaking to you? What action will you take in light of today's devotion?

#DontDoLifeAloneDevo #ReadPrayApplyRemain

Ezekiel 31:1-32:32, Psalms 113:1-114:8, Proverbs 27:18-20, Hebrews 12:14-29

November 16

"Jesus Christ is the same yesterday, today, and forever." Hebrews 13:8

When everything else falls apart, we still have something to hold on to that remains consistent. His name is Jesus. God has always been faithful and that won't change.

Thank you God for another day and for your word. Help me process it, live it and share it. In Jesus' name I pray, amen.

What is God speaking to you? What action will you take in light of today's devotion?

#DontDoLifeAloneDevo #ReadPrayApplyRemain

Ezekiel 33:1-34:31, Psalms 115:1-18, Proverbs 27:21-22, Hebrews 13:1-25

November 17

"If any of you lacks wisdom, let him ask of God, who gives to all liberally and without reproach, and it will be given to him." James 1:5

We seek out information from so many different sources, but none of them will keep showing up in our life the way God does. When God is teaching me something, I take notes. Let God lead the way.

Thank you God for another day and for your word. Help me process it, live it and share it. In Jesus' name I pray, amen.

What is God speaking to you? What action will you take in light of today's devotion?

#DontDoLifeAloneDevo #ReadPrayApplyRemain

Ezekiel 35:1-36:38, Psalms 116:1-19, Proverbs 27:23-27, James 1:1-18

November 18

"But be doers of the word, and not hearers only, deceiving yourselves." James 1:22

Information without application does not change anything. God calls us to do something with our faith. Walk it out.

Thank you God for another day and for your word. Help me process it, live it and share it. In Jesus' name I pray, amen.

What is God speaking to you? What action will you take in light of today's devotion?

#DontDoLifeAloneDevo #ReadPrayApplyRemain

Ezekiel 37:1-38:23, Psalms 117:1-2, Proverbs 28:1, James 1:19-2:17

November 19

"Does a spring send forth fresh water and bitter from the same opening?" James 3:11

The things we say will eventually reveal the depths of our heart. If you don't like the output, change the input. Fresh springs produce fresh water. Let the same be true of the words that we say.

Thank you God for another day and for your word. Help me process it, live it and share it. In Jesus' name I pray, amen.

What is God speaking to you? What action will you take in light of today's devotion?

#DontDoLifeAloneDevo #ReadPrayApplyRemain

Ezekiel 39:1-40:27, Psalms 118:1-18, Proverbs 28:2, James 2:18-3:18

November 20

"Whereas you do not know what will happen tomorrow. For what is your life? It is even a vapor that appears for a little time and then vanishes away." James 4:14

Sometimes we think we have time, but our brother James reminds us here that tomorrow is not promised. Love well, forgive quickly, and be more intentional. Especially when it comes to relationships.

Thank you God for another day and for your word. Help me process it, live it and share it. In Jesus' name I pray, amen.

What is God speaking to you? What action will you take in light of today's devotion?

#DontDoLifeAloneDevo #ReadPrayApplyRemain

Ezekiel 40:28-41:26, Psalms 118:19-29, Proverbs 28:3-5, James 4:1-17

November 21

"Confess your trespasses to one another, and pray for one another, that you may be healed. The effective, fervent prayer of a righteous man avails much." James 5:16

We can go to God for forgiveness, but here we see that we can find healing through our relationships. God uses people to help us along the way. Don't do life alone.

Thank you God for another day and for your word. Help me process it, live it and share it. In Jesus' name I pray, amen.

What is God speaking to you? What action will you take in light of today's devotion?

#DontDoLifeAloneDevo #ReadPrayApplyRemain

Ezekiel 42:1-43:27, Psalms 119:1-16, Proverbs 28:6-7, James 5:1-20

November 22

"Whoever causes the upright to go astray in an evil way, he himself will fall into his own pit; But the blameless will inherit good." Proverbs 28:10

Our life impacts others. Let's live in a way that leaves other people better off.

Thank you God for another day and for your word. Help me process it, live it and share it. In Jesus' name I pray, amen.

What is God speaking to you? What action will you take in light of today's devotion?

#DontDoLifeAloneDevo #ReadPrayApplyRemain

Ezekiel 44:1-45:12, Psalms 119:17-32, Proverbs 28:8-10, 1 Peter 1:1-12

November 23

"But you are a chosen generation, a royal priesthood, a holy nation, His own special people, that you may proclaim the praises of Him who called you out of darkness into His marvelous light;" I Peter 2:9

God created you, loves you and chose you to do incredible things. The work that God has done and is doing in our life is not just about us or for us. Share it!

Thank you God for another day and for your word. Help me process it, live it and share it. In Jesus' name I pray, amen.

What is God speaking to you? What action will you take in light of today's devotion?

#DontDoLifeAloneDevo #ReadPrayApplyRemain

Ezekiel 45:13-46:24, Psalms 119:33-48, Proverbs 28:11, 1 Peter 1:13-2:10

November 24

"He who covers his sins will not prosper, but whoever confesses and forsakes them will have mercy." Proverbs 28:13

Regardless of how we get there, sin takes us further than we want to go, costs us more than we want to pay and keeps us longer than we want to stay. God is not trying to keep us from good things. He's trying to keep us for better things.

Thank you God for another day and for your word. Help me process it, live it and share it. In Jesus' name I pray, amen.

What is God speaking to you? What action will you take in light of today's devotion?

#DontDoLifeAloneDevo #ReadPrayApplyRemain

Ezekiel 47:1-48:35, Psalms 119:49-64, Proverbs 28:12-13, 1 Peter 2:11-3:7

November 25

"But in your hearts revere Christ as Lord. Always be prepared to give an answer to everyone who asks you to give the reason for the hope that you have. But do this with gentleness and respect," 1 Peter 3:15

The world needs to hear your story. God is working in your life and the people around you need the hope that you have. Let them know about the goodness of God.

Thank you God for another day and for your word. Help me process it, live it and share it. In Jesus' name I pray, amen.

What is God speaking to you? What action will you take in light of today's devotion?

#DontDoLifeAloneDevo #ReadPrayApplyRemain

Daniel 1:1-2:23, Psalms 119:65-80, Proverbs 28:14, 1 Peter 3:8-4:6

November 26

"Each of you should use whatever gift you have received to serve others, as faithful stewards of God's grace in its various forms." 1 Peter 4:10

If you have ever wanted to make a positive impact in the world, there has never been a better time than right now to serve. People are hurting and looking for hope. The world needs what you bring to the table.

Thank you God for another day and for your word. Help me process it, live it and share it. In Jesus' name I pray, amen.

What is God speaking to you? What action will you take in light of today's devotion?

#DontDoLifeAloneDevo #ReadPrayApplyRemain

Daniel 2:24-3:30, Psalms 119:81-96, Proverbs 28:15-16, 1 Peter 4:7-5:14

November 27

"His divine power has given us everything we need for a godly life through our knowledge of him who called us by his own glory and goodness." 2 Peter 1:3

With God we have all we need to be who He called us to be and walk out our full potential. Walking by faith is not always easy, but it will always be worth it.

Thank you God for another day and for your word. Help me process it, live it and share it. In Jesus' name I pray, amen.

What is God speaking to you? What action will you take in light of today's devotion?

#DontDoLifeAloneDevo #ReadPrayApplyRemain

Daniel 4:1-37, Psalms 119:97-112, Proverbs 28:17-18, 2 Peter 1:1-21

November 28

"Those who work their land will have abundant food, but those who chase fantasies will have their fill of poverty." Proverbs 28:19

I once heard a pastor say that we need to pray like it depends on God but work like it depends on us. Sometimes even waiting on God requires us to work while we wait. Do the best you can with what you have where you are.

Thank you God for another day and for your word. Help me process it, live it and share it. In Jesus' name I pray, amen.

What is God speaking to you? What action will you take in light of today's devotion?

#DontDoLifeAloneDevo #ReadPrayApplyRemain

Daniel 5:1-31, Psalms 119:113-128, Proverbs 28:19-20, 2 Peter 2:1-22

November 29

"The Lord is not slow in keeping his promise, as some understand slowness. Instead he is patient with you, not wanting anyone to perish, but everyone to come to repentance." 2 Peter 3:9

Jesus came to seek and to save the lost. He wants everyone to know the love and hope that only comes from God. Found people find people. Redeemed people reach people.

Thank you God for another day and for your word. Help me process it, live it and share it. In Jesus' name I pray, amen.

What is God speaking to you? What action will you take in light of today's devotion?

#DontDoLifeAloneDevo #ReadPrayApplyRemain

Daniel 6:1-28, Psalms 119:129-152, Proverbs 28:21-22, 2 Peter 3:1-18

November 30

"If we confess our sins, He is faithful and just to forgive us our sins and to cleanse us from all unrighteousness." I John 1:9

God can make all things new. Jesus did not die on the cross to make bad people good. He died and rose again to bring spiritually dead people to life! He's ready when you are.

Thank you God for another day and for your word. Help me process it, live it and share it. In Jesus' name I pray, amen.

What is God speaking to you? What action will you take in light of today's devotion?

#DontDoLifeAloneDevo #ReadPrayApplyRemain

Daniel 7:1-28, Psalms 119:153-176, Proverbs 28:23-24, 1 John 1:1-10

December 1

"He who is of a proud heart stirs up strife, but he who trusts in the Lord will be prospered."
Proverbs 28:25

Our pride can get in the way and cause harm. Gratitude keeps us humble. If we are full of ourselves, there is no room for God, others or growth. Humble pie has zero calories.

Thank you God for another day and for your word. Help me process it, live it and share it. In Jesus' name I pray, amen.

What is God speaking to you? What action will you take in light of today's devotion?

#DontDoLifeAloneDevo #ReadPrayApplyRemain

Daniel 8:1-27, Psalms 120:1-7, Proverbs 28:25-26, 1 John 2:1-17

December 2

"My help comes from the Lord, who made heaven and earth." Psalms 121:2

We put our trust in things that can let us down all the time. Even people with the best intentions will miss it from time to time. But my help comes from the Lord. He has never failed me.

Thank you God for another day and for your word. Help me process it, live it and share it. In Jesus' name I pray, amen.

What is God speaking to you? What action will you take in light of today's devotion?

#DontDoLifeAloneDevo #ReadPrayApplyRemain

Daniel 9:1-11:1, Psalms 121:1-8, Proverbs 28:27-28, 1 John 2:18-3:6

December 3

"Dear children, let us not love with words or speech but with actions and in truth." 1 John 3:18

In the early 90s there was a song that came out titled, Love is a Verb. A verb is a word used to describe an action. It's good to talk it out, but we need to walk it out. Don't just tell someone you love them. Show them.

Thank you God for another day and for your word. Help me process it, live it and share it. In Jesus' name I pray, amen.

What is God speaking to you? What action will you take in light of today's devotion?

#DontDoLifeAloneDevo #ReadPrayApplyRemain

Daniel 11:2-35, Psalms 122:1-9, Proverbs 29:1, 1 John 3:7-24

December 4

"We love Him because He first loved us." I John 4:19

We can love because He first loved us. We are blessed to be a blessing. If your life is all about you, you are missing out on the best part. We should live in a way that reflects and responds to what God has already done for us.

Thank you God for another day and for your word. Help me process it, live it and share it. In Jesus' name I pray, amen.

What is God speaking to you? What action will you take in light of today's devotion?

#DontDoLifeAloneDevo #ReadPrayApplyRemain

Daniel 11:36-12:13, Psalms 123:1-4, Proverbs 29:2-4, 1 John 4:1-21

December 5

""If it had not been the Lord who was on our side," Let Israel now say—" Psalms 124:1

We don't always realize it, but we have all had so many, if it had not been for the Lord moments. Take some time to reflect on that. It gives a whole new perspective on life.

Thank you God for another day and for your word. Help me process it, live it and share it. In Jesus' name I pray, amen.

What is God speaking to you? What action will you take in light of today's devotion?

#DontDoLifeAloneDevo #ReadPrayApplyRemain

Hosea 1:1-3:5, Psalms 124:1-8, Proverbs 29:5-8, 1 John 5:1-21

December 6

"Those who trust in the Lord are like Mount Zion, which cannot be moved, but abides forever." Psalms 125:1

When we hold on to something that is secure, it makes us more secure. There is nothing more solid or consistent to stay connected to in this ever-changing world like Jesus. You can trust Him.

Thank you God for another day and for your word. Help me process it, live it and share it. In Jesus' name I pray, amen.

What is God speaking to you? What action will you take in light of today's devotion?

#DontDoLifeAloneDevo #ReadPrayApplyRemain

Hosea 4:1-5:15, Psalms 125:1-5, Proverbs 29:9-11, 2 John 1:1-13

December 7

"Dear friend, I pray that you may enjoy good health and that all may go well with you, even as your soul is getting along well." 3 John 1:2

Externally things may be going well, but that may not always be true for the depths of who we are. Slow down long enough to ask yourself how you are really doing. Then let God lead you towards a healthier pace and healing.

Thank you God for another day and for your word. Help me process it, live it and share it. In Jesus' name I pray, amen.

What is God speaking to you? What action will you take in light of today's devotion?

#DontDoLifeAloneDevo #ReadPrayApplyRemain

Hosea 6:1-9:17, Psalms 126:1-6, Proverbs 29:12-14, 3 John 1:1-15

December 8

"Unless the Lord builds the house, they labor in vain who build it; Unless the Lord guards the city, the watchman stays awake in vain." Psalms 127:1

Don't just acknowledge God on occasion with your life. Let God be the foundation for your life. He is better at being God than we ever could be.

Thank you God for another day and for your word. Help me process it, live it and share it. In Jesus' name I pray, amen.

What is God speaking to you? What action will you take in light of today's devotion?

#DontDoLifeAloneDevo #ReadPrayApplyRemain

Hosea 10:1-14:9, Psalms 127:1-5, Proverbs 29:15-17, Jude 1:1-25

December 9

"Where there is no revelation, people cast off restraint; but blessed is the one who heeds wisdom's instruction." Proverbs 29:18

Having a plan or casting vision is important, but information does not change anything without application. God's plan is always better. Listen and take notes.

Thank you God for another day and for your word. Help me process it, live it and share it. In Jesus' name I pray, amen.

What is God speaking to you? What action will you take in light of today's devotion?

#DontDoLifeAloneDevo #ReadPrayApplyRemain

Joel 1:1-3:21, Psalms 128:1-6, Proverbs 29:18, Revelation 1:1-20

December 10

"Remember therefore from where you have fallen; repent and do the first works, or else I will come to you quickly and remove your lamp stand from its place—unless you repent." Revelation 2:5

After telling the church at Ephesus that they have left their first love, they are given an invitation to start over. We serve a God of reconciliation and redemption. Jesus is not finished with your story. It's not too late to begin again.

Thank you God for another day and for your word. Help me process it, live it and share it. In Jesus' name I pray, amen.

What is God speaking to you? What action will you take in light of today's devotion?

#DontDoLifeAloneDevo #ReadPrayApplyRemain

Amos 1:1-3:15, Psalms 129:1-8, Proverbs 29:19-20, Revelation 2:1-17

December 11

"I wait for the Lord, my soul waits, and in His word I do hope." Psalms 130:5

Waiting is hard, but waiting on God to lead us or move in some capacity is always worth it. He is better at being God than we ever could be.

Thank you God for another day and for your word. Help me process it, live it and share it. In Jesus' name I pray, amen.

What is God speaking to you? What action will you take in light of today's devotion?

#DontDoLifeAloneDevo #ReadPrayApplyRemain

Amos 4:1-6:14, Psalms 130:1-8, Proverbs 29:21-22, Revelation 2:18-3:6

December 12

""I know your works. See, I have set before you an open door, and no one can shut it; for you have a little strength, have kept My word, and have not denied My name." Revelation 3:8

When you trust God to lead, He will handle the details. He knows which doors to open and shut, and exactly how to get you where you need to be.

Thank you God for another day and for your word. Help me process it, live it and share it. In Jesus' name I pray, amen.

What is God speaking to you? What action will you take in light of today's devotion?

#DontDoLifeAloneDevo #ReadPrayApplyRemain

Amos 7:1-9:15, Psalms 131:1-3, Proverbs 29:23, Revelation 3:7-22

December 13

"The fear of man brings a snare, but whoever trusts in the Lord shall be safe." Proverbs 29:25

If we are not intentional, we will put expectations on other people that are unrealistic. Not only expectations, but power. Don't fear people. Trust the Lord.

Thank you God for another day and for your word. Help me process it, live it and share it. In Jesus' name I pray, amen.

What is God speaking to you? What action will you take in light of today's devotion?

#DontDoLifeAloneDevo #ReadPrayApplyRemain

Obadiah 1:1-21, Psalms 132:1-18, Proverbs 29:24-25, Revelation 4:1-11

December 14

"How good and pleasant it is when God's people live together in unity!" Psalms 133:1

Relationships matter. There is no better model of unity or community than the Father, Son and Holy Spirit. If we make Jesus the main thing, everything else will fall into place.

Thank you God for another day and for your word. Help me process it, live it and share it. In Jesus' name I pray, amen.

What is God speaking to you? What action will you take in light of today's devotion?

#DontDoLifeAloneDevo #ReadPrayApplyRemain

Jonah 1:1-4:11, Psalms 133:1-3, Proverbs 29:26-27, Revelation 5:1-14

December 15

"The one who breaks open will come up before them; They will break out, pass through the gate, and go out by it; Their king will pass before them, with the Lord at their head.""
Micah 2:13

This verse speaks of God restoring Israel, but He can do the same in your life. God can break off the chains of bondage, break through the things or situations that stand in the way of His plan for your life and restore you.

Thank you God for another day and for your word. Help me process it, live it and share it. In Jesus' name I pray, amen.

What is God speaking to you? What action will you take in light of today's devotion?

#DontDoLifeAloneDevo #ReadPrayApplyRemain

Micah 1:1-4:13, Psalms 134:1-3, Proverbs 30:1-4, Revelation 6:1-17

December 16

"He has shown you, O man, what is good; And what does the Lord require of you but to do justly, to love mercy, and to walk humbly with your God?" Micah 6:8

Our faith is not just about our thoughts or words, but the things we actually do. This is an invitation to attach action with our faith. That's why James 1:22 reminds us to be doers of the word, and not hearers only.

Thank you God for another day and for your word. Help me process it, live it and share it. In Jesus' name I pray, amen.

What is God speaking to you? What action will you take in light of today's devotion?

#DontDoLifeAloneDevo #ReadPrayApplyRemain

Micah 5:1-7:20, Psalms 135:1-21, Proverbs 30:5-6, Revelation 7:1-17

December 17

"Who remembered us in our lowly state, for His mercy endures forever;" Psalms 136:23

God will change our lives for the better if we let Him. He loves us too much to leave us as we are, but He still takes us as we are. Nobody leans into brokenness and brings restoration like Jesus does.

Thank you God for another day and for your word. Help me process it, live it and share it. In Jesus' name I pray, amen.

What is God speaking to you? What action will you take in light of today's devotion?

#DontDoLifeAloneDevo #ReadPrayApplyRemain

Nahum 1:1-3:19, Psalms 136:1-26, Proverbs 30:7-9, Revelation 8:1-13

December 18

"Then the Lord answered me and said: "Write the vision And make it plain on tablets, that he may run who reads it." Habakkuk 2:2

Sometimes God gives us ideas or shows us things. I learned this lesson a long time ago. When God speaks, I take notes.

Thank you God for another day and for your word. Help me process it, live it and share it. In Jesus' name I pray, amen.

What is God speaking to you? What action will you take in light of today's devotion?

#DontDoLifeAloneDevo #ReadPrayApplyRemain

Habakkuk 1:1-3:19, Psalms 137:1-9, Proverbs 30:10, Revelation 9:1-21

December 19

"The Lord your God in your midst, The Mighty One, will save; He will rejoice over you with gladness, He will quiet you with His love, He will rejoice over you with singing."" Zephaniah 3:17

This verse has always been so comforting to me. It is a great reminder that God is with us, and He is more mindful of us than we realize.

Thank you God for another day and for your word. Help me process it, live it and share it. In Jesus' name I pray, amen.

What is God speaking to you? What action will you take in light of today's devotion?

#DontDoLifeAloneDevo #ReadPrayApplyRemain

Zephaniah 1:1-3:20, Psalms 138:1-8, Proverbs 30:11-14, Revelation 10:1-11

December 20

"I will praise You, for I am fearfully and wonderfully made; Marvelous are Your works, and that my soul knows very well." Psalms 139:14

Your value is not found in what you do, but what you do is valuable. Beauty is not found only in how you look, but you were fearfully and wonderfully made by a God that makes beautiful things.

Thank you God for another day and for your word. Help me process it, live it and share it. In Jesus' name I pray, amen.

What is God speaking to you? What action will you take in light of today's devotion?

#DontDoLifeAloneDevo #ReadPrayApplyRemain

Haggai 1:1-2:23, Psalms 139:1-24, Proverbs 30:15-16, Revelation 11:1-19

December 21

"I know that the Lord will maintain the cause of the afflicted, and justice for the poor." Psalms 140:12

God is always fighting for the overlooked, oppressed and underserved. And He has called us to do the same. Our life is not just about us.

Thank you God for another day and for your word. Help me process it, live it and share it. In Jesus' name I pray, amen.

What is God speaking to you? What action will you take in light of today's devotion?

#DontDoLifeAloneDevo #ReadPrayApplyRemain

Zechariah 1:1-21, Psalms 140:1-13, Proverbs 30:17, Revelation 12:1-17

December 22

"Set a guard over my mouth, Lord; keep watch over the door of my lips." Psalms 141:3

There is so much power in the words that we use. They can be helpful or harmful, life-giving or life-taking. Speak life!

Thank you God for another day and for your word. Help me process it, live it and share it. In Jesus' name I pray, amen.

What is God speaking to you? What action will you take in light of today's devotion?

#DontDoLifeAloneDevo #ReadPrayApplyRemain

Zechariah 2:1-3:10, Psalms 141:1-10, Proverbs 30:18-20, Revelation 13:1-18

December 23

"For who has despised the day of small things? For these seven rejoice to see The plumb line in the hand of Zerubbabel. They are the eyes of the Lord, Which scan to and fro throughout the whole earth."" Zechariah 4:10

Sometimes the most seemingly insignificant things end up being critically important. Don't discount small things or small beginnings. Plenty of massive doors in important places hang on small hinges.

Thank you God for another day and for your word. Help me process it, live it and share it. In Jesus' name I pray, amen.

What is God speaking to you? What action will you take in light of today's devotion?

#DontDoLifeAloneDevo #ReadPrayApplyRemain

Zechariah 4:1-5:11, Psalms 142:1-7, Proverbs 30:21-23, Revelation 14:1-20

December 24

"The ants are a people not strong, yet they prepare their food in the summer;"
Proverbs 30:25

The verse before this one recognizes this move by the ants to prepare as exceedingly wise. In what area of your life could you prepare? Is there something that God wants you to step out in faith with to get ready for what He wants to do in or through your life?

Thank you God for another day and for your word. Help me process it, live it and share it. In Jesus' name I pray, amen.

What is God speaking to you? What action will you take in light of today's devotion?

#DontDoLifeAloneDevo #ReadPrayApplyRemain

Zechariah 6:1-7:14, Psalms 143:1-12, Proverbs 30:24-28, Revelation 15:1-8

December 25

"Lord, what is man, that You take knowledge of him? Or the son of man, that You are mindful of him?" Psalms 144:3

The God that created the world, the first and the last, the same yesterday, today and forever loves you and me. It's one thing to believe in God. It's a completely different thing to realize that He loves us and believes in us.

Thank you God for another day and for your word. Help me process it, live it and share it. In Jesus' name I pray, amen.

What is God speaking to you? What action will you take in light of today's devotion?

#DontDoLifeAloneDevo #ReadPrayApplyRemain

Zechariah 8:1-23, Psalms 144:1-15, Proverbs 30:29-31, Revelation 16:1-21

December 26

"Every day I will bless You, and I will praise Your name forever and ever." Psalms 145:2

If God never did another thing for us, we would still have plenty to thank Him for! Every new day that we are given is a blessing from the Lord, and another reason to praise Him.

Thank you God for another day and for your word. Help me process it, live it and share it. In Jesus' name I pray, amen.

What is God speaking to you? What action will you take in light of today's devotion?

#DontDoLifeAloneDevo #ReadPrayApplyRemain

Zechariah 9:1-17, Psalms 145:1-21, Proverbs 30:32, Revelation 17:1-18

December 27

"Do not put your trust in princes, in human beings, who cannot save." Psalms 146:3

People and things will eventually let us down. At some point we will all miss the mark, but God doesn't. He is faithful and trustworthy.

Thank you God for another day and for your word. Help me process it, live it and share it. In Jesus' name I pray, amen.

What is God speaking to you? What action will you take in light of today's devotion?

#DontDoLifeAloneDevo #ReadPrayApplyRemain

Zechariah 10:1-11:17, Psalms 146:1-10, Proverbs 30:33, Revelation 18:1-24

December 28

"He heals the brokenhearted and binds up their wounds." Psalms 147:3

We live in a world that is full of brokenness and pain. But we serve a God that can bring healing and make us whole again.

Thank you God for another day and for your word. Help me process it, live it and share it. In Jesus' name I pray, amen.

What is God speaking to you? What action will you take in light of today's devotion?

#DontDoLifeAloneDevo #ReadPrayApplyRemain

Zechariah 12:1-13:9, Psalms 147:1-20, Proverbs 31:1-7, Revelation 19:1-21

December 29

"Speak up for those who cannot speak for themselves, for the rights of all who are destitute." Proverbs 31:8

Jesus is the perfect example of how to live your life on behalf of others. He lived in obedience to His heavenly father, and came to give His life for us. Jesus even said that the greatest among us would serve others.

Thank you God for another day and for your word. Help me process it, live it and share it. In Jesus' name I pray, amen.

What is God speaking to you? What action will you take in light of today's devotion?

#DontDoLifeAloneDevo #ReadPrayApplyRemain

Zechariah 14:1-21, Psalms 148:1-4, Proverbs 31:8-9, Revelation 20:1-15

December 30

"And God will wipe away every tear from their eyes; there shall be no more death, nor sorrow, nor crying. There shall be no more pain, for the former things have passed away.""
Revelation 21:4

What an incredible promise! Scripture gives us a glimpse of what eternity with Jesus will be like. Our journey through this life may not always be easy, but it's going to be worth it all.

Thank you God for another day and for your word. Help me process it, live it and share it. In Jesus' name I pray, amen.

What is God speaking to you? What action will you take in light of today's devotion?

#DontDoLifeAloneDevo #ReadPrayApplyRemain

Malachi 1:1-2:17, Psalms 149:1-9, Proverbs 31:10-24, Revelation 21:1-27

December 31

"Let everything that has breath praise the Lord,
Praise the Lord!" Psalms 150:6

God's hope for all of us is that we would know
the love of God, and live a life of praise in
response to that love because of the hope and
salvation that we have received through Jesus.

Thank you God for another day and for your
word. Help me process it, live it and share it. In
Jesus' name I pray, amen.

What is God speaking to you? What action will
you take in light of today's devotion?

#DontDoLifeAloneDevo #ReadPrayApplyRemain

Malachi 3:1-4:6, Psalms 150:1-6, Proverbs
31:25-31, Revelation 22:1-21

February 29 Bonus Leap Year Day

"Come to Me, all you who labor and are heavy laden, and I will give you rest. Take My yoke upon you and learn from Me, for I am gentle and lowly in heart, and you will find rest for your souls. For My yoke is easy and My burden is light." Matthew 11:28-30

What do you need to release into God's hands? Fear will hinder us more than failure ever will. Sometimes we hold onto things because we are afraid to let go of what feels comfortable. You can't fully embrace what God has for you if your hands are full.

Thank you God for another day and for your word. Help me process it, live it and share it. In Jesus' name I pray, amen.

What is God speaking to you? What action will you take in light of today's devotion?

#DontDoLifeAloneDevo #ReadPrayApplyRemain

If this devotional book was helpful at all, I would love for you to go on Amazon and write a review. Then send me a message to let me know your thoughts! Visit dontdolifealone.com or send an email to whygoalone@gmail.com. I'd love to hear from you.

- jimmy

Check out other books by Jimmy on Amazon.

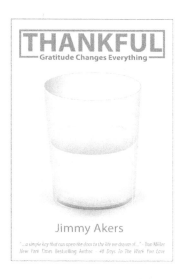

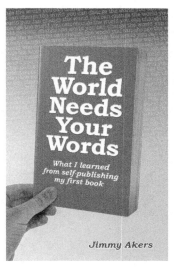

Made in the USA
Middletown, DE
02 January 2023

20971401R00215